GOOD NEWS

THE BEST RELIGION WRITING IN NORTH AMERICA

Edited by Debra A. Wagner

A compilation of religion news writing
recognized for excellence by
Associated Church Press
and published by

SEABURY BOOKS
an imprint of
CHURCH PUBLISHING, NEW YORK

Copyright © 2006 by Associated Church Press.

All rights reserved.

Library of Congress Cataloging-in-Publication Data

Good news : the best religion writing in North America / edited by Debra A. Wagner.
    p. cm.
  ISBN-13: 978-1-59627-028-2
  ISBN-10: 1-59627-028-4
  1. Christian literature – North America. I. Wagner, Debra A.
BR50.G555 2006
277.3′083 – dc22

                                            2006029166

Church Publishing Incorporated
445 Fifth Avenue
New York, NY 10016
www.churchpublishing.org

5 4 3 2 1

Contents

Permissions		ix
1.	Gospel Glory *Cornelius Plantinga Jr.* Reprinted from *The Banner*	3
2.	Black Leather on White Walls: A Church Pays a Small Price for Redeemed Souls *Daniel Lawrence* Reprinted from *Alliance Life*	9
3.	Democracy in the Balance *Bill Moyers* Reprinted from *Sojourners*	13
4.	7 Habits of Highly Effective Mass-Goers *David Philippart* Reprinted from *U.S. Catholic*	25
5.	Irshad Manji *Stephen Swecker* Reprinted from *Zion's Herald*	35
6.	The Lonely Road of Matty Wilson *David Wilson* Reprinted from *The United Church Observer*	44
7.	A Watch of Love: Instructions for Keeping a Vigil of Life with a Loved One Who Is Dying *Walter Friesen* Reprinted from *The Mennonite*	55

8.	Via Media Groups Unite in Atlanta Meeting *Jan Nunley* Reprinted from Episcopal News Service	59
9.	Jesus Cast Out the Demons, Not the People *Lillian Daniel* Reprinted from *DisciplesWorld*	63
10.	Pieta: Colombian Mother Cries for Activist Son Accused of Terrorism *Alexa Smith* Reprinted from Presbyterian News Service	67
11.	Revival Turns Longstanding Rupture into Reconciliation *Andrea Higgins* Reprinted from *Baptist Press News*	72
12.	When It Comes to Music, Christian Teens, Too, Are Pirates *Adelle M. Banks* Reprinted from Religion News Service.	77
13.	Politics and Polarization *Walt Wiltschek* Reprinted from *Messenger*	81
14.	Hearts & Minds: The Power of Reconciliation *Jim Wallis* Reprinted from *Sojourners*	84
15.	Deciphering the Passion: A Guide to What's Biblical and What's Not in Mel Gibson's Movie *Scot McKnight* Reprinted from *The Covenant Companion*	88
16.	Adventist Church Joins Coalition against Worldwide Human Trafficking *Sandra Blackmer* Reprinted from the *Adventist Review*	94

17.	A Conservative Case for Gay Marriage *Rev. Matt Fitzgerald* Reprinted from *Christian Networks Journal*	98
18.	Treasures without Turmoil: Readers Advise How to Distribute Heirlooms after a Family Death *Julie B. Sevig* Reprinted from *The Lutheran*	103
19.	An Answer for Everything? *John Longhurst* Reprinted from the *Mennonite Weekly Review*	109
20.	UMC Panel Condemns Racism at Iliff *Susan Scheib* Reprinted from the *United Methodist Reporter*	112
21.	Front-Page News *Thomas C. Willadsen* Reprinted from *The Cresset*	117
22.	"King of Pop" More Like a "God": Our Adulation for Michael Jackson Unstinting *David W. Reid* Reprinted from *Vital Theology*	121
23.	Eager for Education *Marla Pierson Lester* Reprinted from *A Common Place*	125
24.	Pottery-Making Rare in State Baptist Churches *Sandra Bearden* Reprinted from *The Baptist*	130
25.	How Blind I Was *Sharon Sheridan* Reprinted from *Episcopal Life*	133
26.	Q&A *James Ayers* Reprinted from *Presbyterians Today*	136

27. Why It Was Impossible for Us to Sign Declaration　　138
　　　Leanne Larmondin
　　Reprinted from *The Anglican Journal*

28. Finding the Way Home　　141
　　　Ingrid Christiansen
　　Reprinted from *Lutheran Woman Today*

29. CBS, NBC Refuse to Air Church's Television　　147
　　Advertisement: United Church of Christ Ad
　　Highlighting Jesus' Extravagant Welcome Called
　　"Too Controversial"
　　　J. Bennett Guess
　　Reprinted from *United Church News*

About This Book　　151

Permissions

"Gospel Glory" by Cornelius Plantinga Jr. is reprinted with permission from *The Banner*. Copyright © 2004 CRC Publications. All rights reserved.

"Black Leather on White Walls: A Church Pays a Small Price for Redeemed Souls" by Daniel Lawrence is reprinted with permission from *Alliance Life*. Copyright © 2004 *Alliance Life*. All rights reserved.

"Democracy in the Balance" by Bill Moyers is reprinted with permission from *Sojourners*. Copyright © 2004 Sojourners. *www.sojo.net*. All rights reserved.

"7 Habits of Highly Effective Mass-Goers" by David Philippart is reprinted with permission from *U.S. Catholic*. Copyright © 2004 *U.S. Catholic*. All rights reserved.

"Irshad Manji" by Stephen Swecker is reprinted with permission from *Zion's Herald*. Copyright © 2004 *Zion's Herald*. All rights reserved.

"The Lonely Road of Matty Wilson" by David Wilson is reprinted from *The United Church Observer*. Copyright © 2004 by the author. All rights reserved.

"A Watch of Love: Instructions for Keeping a Vigil of Life with a Loved One Who Is Dying" by Walter Friesen is reprinted with permission from *The Mennonite*. Copyright © 2004 *The Mennonite*. All rights reserved.

"Via Media Groups Unite in Atlanta Meeting" by Jan Nunley is reprinted with permission from Episcopal News Service. Copyright © 2004 The Episcopal Church, USA. Episcopal News Service content may be reprinted without permission as long as credit is given to ENS.

"Jesus Cast Out the Demons, Not the People" by Lillian Daniel is reprinted with permission from *DisciplesWorld*. Copyright © 2004 *Disciples World*. All rights reserved.

"Pieta: Colombian Mother Cries for Activist Son Accused of Terrorism" by Alexa Smith is reprinted with permission from Presbyterian News Service. Copyright © 2004 Presbyterian News Service. All rights reserved.

"Revival Turns Longstanding Rupture into Reconciliation" by Andrea Higgins is reprinted with permission from Baptist Press News. Copyright © 2004 Southern Baptist Convention, Baptist Press. All rights reserved.

"When It Comes to Music, Christian Teens, Too, Are Pirates" by Adelle M. Banks is reprinted with permission from Religion News Service. Copyright © 2004 Religion News Service. All rights reserved.

"Politics and Polarization" by Walt Wiltschek is reprinted with permission from the *Messenger*. Copyright © 2004 Church of the Brethren. All rights reserved.

"Hearts & Minds: The Power of Reconciliation" by Jim Wallis is reprinted with permission from *Sojourners*. Copyright © 2004 *Sojourners*. www.sojo.net. All rights reserved.

"Deciphering the Passion: A Guide to What's Biblical and What's Not in Mel Gibson's Movie" by Scot McKnight is reprinted with permission from *The Covenant Companion*. Copyright © 2004 *The Covenant Companion*. All rights reserved.

Permissions

"Adventist Church Joins Coalition against Worldwide Human Trafficking" by Sandra Blackmer is reprinted with permission from *Adventist Review*. Copyright © 2004 *Adventist Review*. All rights reserved.

"A Conservative Case for Gay Marriage" by Matt Fitzgerald is reprinted with permission from *Christian Networks Journal*. Copyright © 2004 *Christian Networks Journal*. All rights reserved.

"Treasures without Turmoil: Readers Advise How to Distribute Heirlooms after a Family Death" by Julie B. Sevig is reprinted with permission from *The Lutheran*. Copyright © 2004 Augsburg Fortress. All rights reserved.

"An Answer for Everything?" by John Longhurst is reprinted with permission from *Mennonite Weekly Review*. Copyright © 2004 Mennonite Weekly Review Inc. All rights reserved.

"UMC Panel Condemns Racism at Iliff" by Susan Scheib is reprinted with permission from *United Methodist Reporter*. Copyright © 2004 UMR Communications. All rights reserved.

"Front-Page News" by Thomas C. Willadsen is reprinted with permission from *The Cresset*. Copyright © 2004 Valparaiso University Press. All rights reserved.

"Eager for Education" by Marla Pierson Lester is reprinted with permission from *A Common Place*. Copyright © 2004 Mennonite Central Committee. All rights reserved.

"Pottery-Making Rare in State Baptist Churches" by Sandra Bearden is reprinted with permission from *The Alabama Baptist*. Copyright © 2004 *The Alabama Baptist*. All rights reserved.

"How Blind I Was" by Sharon Sheridan is reprinted with permission from *Episcopal Life*. Copyright © 2004 *Episcopal Life*. All rights reserved.

"Q&A" by James Ayers is reprinted with permission from *Presbyterians Today*. Copyright © 2004 Presbyterian Church (U.S.A.). All rights reserved.

"Why It Was Impossible for Us to Sign Declaration" by Leanne Larmondin is reprinted with permission from *The Anglican Journal*. Copyright © 2004 The Anglican Church of Canada. All rights reserved.

"Finding the Way Home" by Ingrid Christiansen is reprinted with permission from *Lutheran Woman Today*. Copyright © 2004 Women of the Evangelical Lutheran Church in America. All rights reserved.

"CBS, NBC Refuse to Air Church's Television Advertisement: United Church of Christ Ad Highlighting Jesus' Extravagant Welcome Called 'Too Controversial' " by J. Bennett Guess is reprinted with permission from United Church News. Copyright © 2004 United Church News. All rights reserved.

GOOD NEWS

1

Gospel Glory
Cornelius Plantinga Jr.

Viktor Klemperer was professor of literature at the University of Dresden during the years that led into World War II, and he had the job he wanted. All his life he had loved to read and write, and all his life he had dreamed of writing the world's best book on 18th-century French literature. If he succeeded, he'd be famous on campuses across the world. He could hold his head up in the faculty lounge. At conferences he could autograph his book, and he could do it graciously and illegibly. He'd be a master in his field! Anybody who wanted to talk about 18th-century French literature would have to talk about Viktor Klemperer!

But then the Nazis came to power and started removing one part of Klemperer's life after another. They took away his telephone and then his car. They canceled some of his courses at the university and then they canceled all of them. The Nazis removed his typewriter and then they took away his house and gave it to a local grocer. (The grocer was actually opposed to Hitler, but he was still pleased to have Klemperer's house.) The Nazis moved Klemperer into a so-called Jews' House, normally the last stop on the way to the camps, and they also killed Klemperer's cat because, of course, Jews could not own pets.

As the Nazis robbed him, Klemperer wrote it all down in his diary. He wrote about his deprivations and the indignities that came with them. He described suffering and what it did to people — how it made

---

Reprinted from *The Banner*.

some of them large-hearted and compassionate, how it made others tight and self-protective. In 1941, after a terrifying run-in with the police, Klemperer opened his diary and wrote these words: "I want to bear witness, precise witness, until the very end." He knew that in his confinement he couldn't write a big history of Nazi cruelty. But he could tell his diary about the ordinary ways the Nazis stripped people of their dignity, right down to the last rag of it.

Viktor Klemperer had hoped to write the world's best account of 18th-century French literature. But the Nazis took his life away.

Except that, at the end of the day, they didn't. They couldn't. Viktor Klemperer's diaries survived and are now celebrated all over the world. My friend Eleanor Stump pointed this out to me one day. Klemperer thought his glory would be a book about French literature, but the Lord meant his glory to be his daily diary. Viktor Klemperer couldn't stop the Nazis from robbing him, but there was one thing he could do. He could "bear witness, precise witness," and he could "bear it to the end." He was a witness to the truth, and he never knew that *this* would be his glory.

Where We're Not Looking

How hard it is to see real glory when we think glory is all about making a splash. We miss the real thing because we get our standards from people who've got glory mixed up with publicity — people like pro athletes and entertainers, hard-charging winners in business who then star in their own TV show. Some folks think there's glory in being lethal, so their idea of great entertainment is a vengeful movie and a tub of popcorn. In ordinary life glory is reputation, and it's built on competition and publicity and peer review by people just as fouled up as we are.

So once more the Bible must be our teacher because it finds glory somewhere else — usually in places we're not looking for it. The gospel of John is especially intriguing in this respect.

In John 2 Jesus goes to a wedding at which his mother reports a wine shortage, so Jesus goes to work. He makes some wine, maybe as much as 150 gallons (must have been a large wedding). And, of course, when it comes to making wine Jesus has an advantage over other vintners because he's the one through whom everything was made in the beginning. Jesus knows his business, so he makes very good wine, special reserve wine that bursts with fruit. The gospel says it was a sign of his glory. We want to know what this mysterious glory is and why we should see it in wine making.

In John 12 death is in the air. The Son of Man will die and fall into the earth in an event so devastating that it will seem to turn creation back into chaos, but Jesus says this is the hour in which the Son of Man will be *glorified*. And we grope for his meaning. How can this be? Getting glorified on a cross? Is that like getting enthroned on an electric chair? Is it like being honored by a firing squad?

Glory in the cross of Jesus Christ sounds almost grotesque. After all, as Jürgen Moltmann once wrote, Jesus was crucified "not between two candles on an altar, but between two thieves in a place named for a skull." Jesus, the friend of sinners, was crucified between his kind of people in a Godforsaken place where all the lights go out from noon to three. Yet the gospel wants us to find glory in this disaster, and we want to know what this mysterious glory is and why we should see it in Jesus' terrible suffering.

John 13 tells us that one night when Jesus' hour had come, he took off his robe, tied a towel around his waist, poured water into a basin, and bent over the feet of his disciples. Jesus did for them what they would never have dreamed of doing for each other, and he did it for Judas too. He also handed Judas bread — *feeding* the traitor, feeding the traitor with *bread*, the staff of life! According to the gospel, when Judas took these gifts from Jesus and walked out into the darkness with them Jesus said, "Now is the Son of Man glorified and God is glorified in him." And once more we want to know what this mysterious glory is all about and why we should find it in the washing and the feeding.

Grace upon Grace

Glory is everywhere in the gospel, and it's got nothing to do with competition or making a splash. The glory is in wine and blood. It's in bread and bath water. It's where we're not looking, but it's certainly where Jesus is, and of course God the Father is mixed up in the glory too because the Son does just what his Father does. He says just what his Father says. The Son is his Father all over again.

If that isn't mystery and glory enough, think of what our Lord says in John 17. Jesus' hour has come. He's only one chapter from the place where Judas and the soldiers will meet him with their torches and weapons. So what does Jesus do? He prays for his disciples. He thinks of *them* and prays for *them*. He thinks even of the next generation of disciples who will be gathered through evangelism, and he prays for them too. Protect them, he prays. Sanctify them. Unite them. Fill them with joy. Let me be in them and you in me and they in us. Let your love, which has been my own life's blood from before the foundation of the world, be in them and I in them — and in all the generations of children who will believe the truth.

The gospel says that after Jesus spoke those words he went out to the garden to meet Judas and the soldiers.

> *Holy Father, protect them. Unite them. Love them. Fill them with joy. Let me be in them.*

The prayer is thrilling in its courage and beauty. And at its center lies an exchange of glory:

> [Jesus] *looked up to heaven and said: "Father, the hour has come. Glorify your Son so that your Son may glorify you."*
>
> *"The glory that you have given me I have given them so that they may be one as we are one."* (17:1, 22)

Jesus pours himself out for his disciples while his own life hangs by a thread, and in this we behold his glory, glory as of the one and only from the Father, full of grace and truth. Here is the fullness of grace, grace upon grace, grace that is always out to bless, to adorn, to unite, to cause others to flourish, grace that is always thinking of others, doing whatever it takes, paying whatever it costs so that they may live and do so abundantly.

His Father All Over Again

Where did Jesus get all this self-spending glory? He got some of it from his mother, didn't he, the fierce and blessed Virgin Mary! Jesus was his mother's Son. He got some of it from the Holy Spirit, who conceived him and descended upon him and remained with him. And, of course, from all eternity Jesus Christ, God's only Son, the Word of God, the light of God — from all eternity Jesus Christ got his glorious self-giving habits from being in the bosom of his Father, the One whose greatness *consists* so much in his goodness.

So Jesus does just what he sees his Father doing. Jesus makes lots of wine at Cana because he comes from a wine-making family. Every fall God turns water into wine in France and Chile and the Napa Valley. Gregory the Great said that at Cana Jesus did a small, sped-up version of what God does all the time in the great vineyards of the world. Jesus makes wine for people because they're at a wedding, and he wants them to flourish there. He wants to make their joy full.

Glory in the wine of Jesus, and glory in the washbasin of Jesus. Hasn't God always humbled himself to serve us, even when our sin has led us into terrible trouble? "Have mercy on me, O God, according to your unfailing love; according to your great compassion.... Wash away all my iniquity and cleanse me from my sin" (Ps. 51:1–2). Jesus, on his knees before his disciples, is doing what he sees his Father doing, and of course the gospel finds glory here because it's so much like God to clean people up.

And bread for a traitor? Doesn't God provide that all the time — sending rain on the fields of the just and the unjust so that their crops will grow and *they* will grow too as they feed on God's gifts? Jesus hands Judas a piece of bread because he does what he sees his Father doing, and the gospel finds glory here because it's so much like God to feed enemies even while opposing their evil.

The gospel finds glory where we're not looking — in wine, water, and bread, even in the blood of Jesus our Savior. In the mystery of the cross, the humiliating death of Jesus Christ was actually a triumph of self-giving love, "the atoning sacrifice for... the sins of the whole world" (1 John 2:2). That's why it brings glory to God. The point is that God's splendor becomes clearer whenever God or the Son of God powerfully spends himself in order to cause others to flourish. This is what makes God eminent in the world. This is the power and the glory.

And it's this glory that Jesus wants to pass on to his disciples. How astonishing it is that when we help others to thrive, when we encourage them, strengthen them, liberate them, keep our promises to them — how astonishing that when we do these things *we are like God!*

We thought we'd get glory by writing a terrific book or getting a strong peer review from people just as foolish as we are. But the Spirit of Truth tells us that real glory is in the wine and the blood and the water and the bread — all signs of mighty self-expenditure by God for people who don't deserve it at all.

Rev. Cornelius Plantinga Jr. is president of Calvin Theological Seminary.

2

Black Leather on White Walls
A Church Pays a Small Price for Redeemed Souls
Daniel Lawrence

She was a "biker chick." In her own words, she "drank too much, did drugs and wasn't a very nice person." On the outside Amy portrayed a biker image; on the inside she wanted and needed a relationship with God. She didn't know where to find it until some friends invited her to a church that would allow bikers to come as they are.

Amy first visited Murrysville Alliance Church (Murrysville, Pa.) on a Sunday when we were having our annual "Blessing of the Bikes" service. After that she started coming every week and began to listen to what God had to say to her.

Several bikers who'd been coming to Murrysville Alliance regularly were surprised that our congregation welcomed them, even when they dressed in leathers. We let them know that they could come no matter what they were wearing.

Eventually they asked if we would hold a Sunday service at the beginning of the biking season to which they could invite their friends and other bikers. The purpose would be to pray for their safety.

At our first Blessing of the Bikes event in 1997, 200 bikers came. Word spread that Murrysville Alliance is a place that's open to bikers, and attendance has grown over the years. In 2003 we had 3,000 bikers and their riders at the church. Motorcycles filled our parking lot and lined the streets, and the police helped direct traffic.

Reprinted from *Alliance Life*.

Open Doors

Each April when it's time for the Blessing of the Bikes, our congregation greets the event with much apprehension. Will it rain? Who will come? How many motorcycles will ride in for the service?

We look forward to seeing old friends whom we may see only on this occasion. Some tell us of their buddies who attended last year but couldn't make it this time because of sickness, hard times or death. Together we reminisce and sometimes pray. The riders come for different reasons, but all receive a prayer for safety as they begin the riding season.

Bikers aren't always sure why we open our doors for them since many churches won't, considering the loud pipes, tattoos, leathers, stickers and pins that express worldly personal views. A few attend only out of curiosity, but most sincerely appreciate that a local church will welcome them on this day and any Sunday they wish to attend.

Count the Cost

There's a price to pay to reach the unchurched and religious wanderers who are seeking truth. Inviting them into the church means the congregation must take a risk. We've learned that in order to see lives changed, the building and all that is in it have to be totally given to God.

Just as kids who come to Vacation Bible School leave dirty fingerprints on the walls, bikers leave kickstand holes in the pavement, cigarette butts on the lawn, odors of nicotine and alcohol in the hallways — and maybe even black leather marks on white walls.

Murrysville Alliance had just moved into a new sanctuary in April 2002, and the Blessing of the Bikes was scheduled for our second Sunday service there. We were excited because more people — double the number from the year before — could come and hear about Jesus Christ.

The day arrived, and orange cones were set up in the parking lot, parking attendants were ready to go and those involved in worship were expecting great things from God. The press even showed up. Then it rained. Literally, it poured.

We knew that our building, with its freshly painted walls, new carpet and renovated bathrooms, was going to take a beating. Bikers showed up completely drenched, looking for shelter and a cup of hot coffee. The only place to go was inside the church.

Before long, mud was everywhere. Bikers' new leathers bled black dye all over the walls — in the halls, bathrooms and wherever our guests stood for any length of time. There was standing room only during the worship service, so one can only imagine what the walls looked like.

I had a sick feeling as I watched abstract paintings of black forming everywhere. Hours of hard work and money were invested in the building. Why did it have to rain, God?

Whose Walls?

At that point God stopped me in my tracks and did His own work of art — in my life. He reminded me that those church walls didn't belong to me. Besides, they could be cleaned or repainted.

God made it clear that it was raining for a reason. These men and women didn't have to come; they wanted to be here. As a result of the rain, bikers came inside and heard a message they wouldn't have heard otherwise. Many came in cars and brought their entire families, which they couldn't do on a motorcycle. We had kids in children's church who never would have been there if it hadn't rained.

After the service I went into the lobby and saw a biker who didn't "do" church. We had been reaching out to him for years. He greeted me with a big hug and told me that he watched the entire service on the monitor. "You stayed for the whole service?" I asked.

He said, "It's raining! I had nowhere else to go." He laughed, shook my hand and walked away. At that moment, black leather marks on white walls were worth it all.

When nonbelievers see the church in worship, it's contagious. Because of that rainy Sunday, several bikers returned, and lives have been changed. Only God knows the eternal differences that were made that day. I learned to let go and give God back His church.

What if we had chosen not to have our carpets soiled and walls marked up? What would have happened if we had decided that the risk was too high and the inconvenience too great? I have often speculated that the reason many Christian biker groups work outside the Church is that they are not permitted to work inside it. Jesus, through the power of His Holy Spirit, wants to use local churches to fulfill the Great Commission.

Getting It Done means opening our doors to those who will, at times, leave black leather on white walls. Isn't it great to know that God will work out not only the black marks on our church walls but also the stains that blacken our hearts? He forgives us and washes us clean.

Our congregation has seen men and women changed forever, diamonds in the rough but nonetheless changed. Jesus will do the same for any one of us. All we have to do is ask (1 John 1:9).

One Sunday when Amy, the biker chick, was at our church, the sermon was on the sinful woman who washed Jesus' feet with her tears (Luke 7:37). When the altar call was given, she was the first one down the aisle. With tears streaming down her face, she gave her life to Jesus.

Life has not been easy for Amy. Many ghosts from her past haunt her every day. In the testimony she gave when she was baptized, she said, "I no longer feel alone. The love that I feel and receive from the Lord is awesome. My life has been turned around. The inner peace I have is a great feeling."

Rev. Daniel Lawrence and his wife, Cindy, live in Murrysville, Pa., where Daniel is pastor of Murrysville Alliance Church.

3

Democracy in the Balance
Bill Moyers

How do we nurture the healing side of religion over the killing side? How do we protect the soul of democracy against bad theology in service of an imperial state?

I trace my spiritual lineage back to a radical Baptist in England named Thomas Helwys who believed that God, and not the King, was Lord of conscience. In 1612 Roman Catholics were the embattled target of the Crown and Thomas Helwys, the Baptist, came to their defense with the first tract in English demanding full religious liberty. Here's what he said:

> Our Lord the King has no more power over their [Catholic] consciences than ours, and that is none at all.... For men's religion is betwixt God and themselves; the King shall not answer it; neither may the King be judge betwixt God and man. Let them be heretics, Turks, Jews, or whatever. It appertains not to the earthly power to punish them in the least measure.

The king was the good King James I — yes, *that* King James, as in the King James Bible. Challenges to his authority did not cause his head to rest easily on his pillow, so James had Thomas Helwys thrown into prison, where he died.

Thomas Helwys was not the first or last dissenter to pay the supreme price for conscience. While we are not called upon in America today to make a similar sacrifice, we are in need of his generous

---

Reprinted from *Sojourners*.

vision of religious freedom. We are heading into a new religious landscape. For most of our history our religious discourse was dominated by white male Protestants of a culturally conservative European heritage, people like me. Dissenting voices of America, alternative visions of faith, race, and gender, rarely reached the mainstream. It's different now. Immigration has added more than 30 million people to our population since the late 1960s. The American gene pool is mutating into one in which people like me will be a minority within half a century.

America is being re-created right before our eyes. The world keeps moving to America, bringing new stories from the four corners of the globe. Gerard Bruns calls it a "contest of narratives" competing to shape a new American drama.

The old story had a paradox at its core. In no small part because of Baptists like Thomas Helwys and other "freethinkers," the men who framed our Constitution believed in religious tolerance in a secular republic. The state was not to choose sides among competing claims of faith. So they embodied freedom of religion in the First Amendment. Another person's belief, said Thomas Jefferson, "neither picks my pocket not breaks my bones." It was a noble sentiment often breached in practice. The Indians who lived here first had more than their pockets picked; the Africans brought here forcibly against their will had more than their bones broken. Even when most Americans claimed a Protestant heritage and practically everyone looked alike, we often failed the tolerance test; Catholics, Jews, and Mormons had to struggle to resist being absorbed without distinction into the giant mix-master of American assimilation.

So our troubled past with tolerance requires us to ask how, in this new era when we are looking even less and less alike, are we to avoid the intolerance, the chauvinism, the fanaticism, the bitter fruits that mark the long history of world religions when they jostle each other in busy, crowded streets?

It is no rhetorical question. My friend Elaine Pagels, the noted scholar of religion, says, "There's practically no religion I know of that sees other people in a way that affirms the other's choice." You only have to glance at the daily news to see how passions are stirred by claims of exclusive loyalty to one's own kin, one's own clan, one's own country, and one's own church. These ties that bind are vital to our communities and our lives, but they can also be twisted into a noose.

Religion has a healing side, but it also has a killing side. In the opening chapter of Genesis — the founding document of three great faiths — the first murder rises from a religious act. You know the story: Adam and Eve become the first parents to discover what it means to raise Cain. God plays favorites and chooses Abel's offering over Cain. Cain is so jealous he strikes out at his brother and kills him. Sibling rivalry for God's favor leads to violence and ends in death.

Once this pattern is established, it's played out in the story of Isaac and Ishmael, Jacob and Esau, Joseph and his brothers, and down through the centuries in generation after generation of conflict between Muslims and Jews, Jews and Christians, Christians and Muslims, so that the red thread of religiously spilled blood runs directly from East of Eden to Bosnia, Beirut, Belfast, and Baghdad.

In our time alone the litany is horrendous. I keep a file marked "Holy War." It bulges with stories of Shias and Sunnis in fratricidal conflict. Of teenage girls in Algeria shot in the face for not wearing a veil. Of professors whose throats are cut for teaching male and female students in the same classroom. Of the fanatical Jewish doctor with a machine gun mowing down 30 praying Muslims in a mosque. Of Muslim suicide bombers bent on the obliteration of Jews. Of the young Orthodox Jew who assassinated Yitzhak Rabin and then announced to the world that "Everything I did, I did for the glory of God." Of Hindus and Muslims slaughtering each other in India, of Christians and Muslims perpetuating gruesome vengeance on each another in Nigeria.

Meanwhile, groups calling themselves the Christian Identity Movement and the Christian Patriot League arm themselves, and Christians intoxicated with the delusional doctrine of two 19th-century preachers not only await the rapture but believe they have an obligation to get involved politically to hasten the divine scenario for the Apocalypse that will bring an end to the world. Sadly, Christians, too, can invoke God for the purpose of waging religious war. "Onward Christian Soldiers" is back in vogue and the 21st century version of the Crusades has taken on aspects of the righteous ferocity that marked its predecessors. "To be furious in religion," said the Quaker William Penn, "is to be furiously irreligious."

This is a time of testing — for people of faith and for people who believe in democracy. How do we nurture the healing side of religion over the killing side? How do we protect the soul of democracy against the contagion of a triumphalist theology in the service of an imperial state? At stake is America's role in the world. At stake is the very character of the American Experiment — whether "we, the people" is the political incarnation of a spiritual truth — one nation, indivisible — or a stupendous fraud.

There are two Americas today. You could see this division in a little-noticed action this spring in the House of Representatives. Republicans in the House approved new tax credits for the children of families earning as much as $309,000 a year — families that already enjoy significant benefits from earlier tax cuts — while doing next to nothing for those at the low end of the income scale. This, said *The Washington Post* in an editorial called "Leave No Rich Child Behind," is "bad social policy, bad tax policy, and bad fiscal policy. You'd think they'd be embarrassed but they're not."

Nothing seems to embarrass the political class in Washington today. Not the fact that more children are growing up in poverty in America than in any other industrial nation; not the fact that millions of workers are actually making less money today in real dollars than they did 20 years ago; not the fact that working people are putting in longer and longer hours just to stay in place; not the fact that while we have the most advanced medical care in the world, nearly 44 million Americans — eight out of 10 of them in working families — are uninsured and cannot get the basic care they need.

Nor is the political class embarrassed by the fact that the gap between rich and poor is greater than it's been in 50 years — the worst inequality among all Western nations. They don't seem to have noticed that we have been experiencing a shift in poverty. For years it was said that single jobless mothers are down there at the bottom. For years it was said that work, education, and marriage is how they move up the economic ladder. But poverty is showing up where we didn't expect it — among families that include two parents, a worker, and a head of the household with more than a high school education. These are the newly poor. These are the people our political and business class expects to climb out of poverty on an escalator moving downward.

For years now a small fraction of American households have been garnering an extreme concentration of wealth and income while large corporations and financial institutions have obtained unprecedented levels of economic and political power over daily life. In 1960, the gap in terms of wealth between the top 20 percent and the bottom 20 percent was 30-fold. Four decades later it is more than 75-fold. Such concentrations of wealth would be far less of an issue if the rest of society was benefiting proportionately and equality was growing. That's not the case. As an organization called The Commonwealth Foundation Center for the Renewal of American Democracy sets forth in well-documented research, working families and the poor "are losing ground under economic pressures that deeply affect household stability, family dynamics, social mobility, political participation, and civic life."

And household economics "is not the only area where inequality is growing in America." We are also losing the historic balance between wealth and commonwealth. The report goes on to describe "a fanatical drive to dismantle the political institutions, the legal and statutory canons, and the intellectual and cultural frameworks that have shaped public responsibility for social harms arising from the excesses of private power." That drive is succeeding, with drastic consequences for an equitable access to and control of public resources, the lifeblood of any democracy. From land, water, and other natural resources to media and the broadcast and digital spectrums, to scientific discovery and medical breakthroughs, and even to politics itself, a broad range of the American commons is undergoing a powerful shift in the direction of private control.

And what is driving this shift? Contrary to what you learned in civics class in high school, it is not the so-called "democratic debate." That is merely a cynical charade behind which the real business goes on — the none-too-scrupulous business of getting and keeping power so that you can divide up the spoils. If you want to know what's changing America, follow the money.

Veteran Washington reporter Elizabeth Drew says, "the greatest change in Washington over the past 25 years — in its culture, in the way it does business and the ever-burgeoning amount of business transactions that go on here — has been in the preoccupation with money." Jeffrey Birnbaum, who covered Washington for nearly 20 years for the *Wall Street Journal,* put it even more strongly: "[Campaign cash] has flooded over the gunwales of the ship of state and threatens to sink the entire vessel. Political donations determine the course and speed of many government actions that deeply affect our daily lives."

It is widely accepted in Washington today that there is nothing wrong with a democracy dominated by the people with money. But of course there is. Money has democracy in a stranglehold and is suffocating it. During his brief campaign in 2000, before he was ambushed by the dirty tricks of the Religious Right in South Carolina and big money from George W. Bush's wealthy elites, John McCain said elections today are nothing less than an "influence peddling scheme in which both parties compete to stay in office by selling the country to the highest bidder."

That's the shame of politics today. The consequences: "When powerful interests shower Washington with millions in campaign contributions, they often get what they want. But it is ordinary citizens and firms that pay the price, and most of them never see it coming," according to *Time* magazine. *Time* concludes that America now has "government for the few at the expense of the many."

That's why so many people are turned off by politics. It's why we can't put things right. *And it's wrong.* Hear the great Justice Learned Hand on this: "If we are to keep our democracy, there must be one commandment: 'Thou shalt not ration justice.' " He got it right: The rich have the right to buy more homes than anyone else. They have the right to buy more cars, more clothes, or more vacations than anyone else. But they don't have the right to buy more democracy than anyone else.

I know: This sounds very much like a call for class war. But the class war was declared a generation ago, in a powerful polemic by a wealthy right-winger, William Simon, who was soon to be Secretary of the Treasury. By the end of the '70s, corporate America had begun a stealthy assault on the rest of our society and the principles of our democracy. Looking backward, it all seems so clear that we wonder how we could have ignored the warning signs at the time.

What has been happening to the middle and working classes is not the result of Adam Smith's invisible hand but the direct consequence of corporate activism, intellectual collusion, the rise of a religious orthodoxy that has made an idol of wealth and power, and a host of political decisions favoring the powerful monied interests who were determined to get back the privileges they had lost with the Depression and the New Deal. They set out to trash the social contract; to cut workforces and their wages; to scour the globe in search of cheap labor; and to shred the social safety net that was supposed to protect people from hardships beyond their control. *Business Week* put it bluntly: "Some people will obviously have to do with less.... It will be a bitter pill for many Americans to swallow the idea of doing with less so that big business can have more."

To create the intellectual framework for this revolution in public policy, they funded conservative think tanks — the Heritage

Foundation, the Hoover Institution, and the American Enterprise Institute — that churned out study after study advocating their agenda.

To put political muscle behind these ideas, they created a formidable political machine. Thomas Edsall of *The Washington Post,* one of the few journalists to cover the issues of class, wrote: "During the 1970s, business refined its ability to act as a class, submerging competitive instincts in favor of joint, cooperative action in the legislative area." Big business political action committees flooded the political arena with a deluge of dollars. And they built alliances with the Religious Right — Jerry Falwell's Moral Majority and Pat Robertson's Christian Coalition — who happily contrived a cultural war as a smokescreen to hide the economic plunder of the very people who were enlisted as foot soldiers in the war.

And they won. Warren Buffett, one of the richest men in America and the savviest investor of them all, put it this way: "If there was a class war, my class won." Well, there was, Mr. Buffett, and as a recent headline in *The Washington Post* proclaimed: "Business Wins With Bush."

Look at the spoils of victory: Over the past three years, they've pushed through $2 trillion dollars in tax cuts. More than half of the benefits are going to the wealthiest 1 percent. You could call it trickle-down economics, except that the only thing that trickled down was a sea of red ink in our state and local governments, forcing them to cut services and raise taxes on middle class working America.

Now the Congressional Budget Office forecasts deficits totaling $2.75 trillion over the next 10 years. These deficits have been part of their strategy. The late Sen. Daniel Patrick Moynihan tried to warn us, when he predicted that President Reagan's real strategy was to force the government to cut domestic social programs by fostering federal deficits of historic dimensions. President Reagan's own budget director, David Stockman, admitted as much. Now the leading right-wing political strategist, Grover Norquist, says the goal is to "starve the beast" — with trillions of dollars in deficits resulting from trillions of dollars in tax cuts, until the U.S. government is so anemic and anorexic it can be drowned in the bathtub.

Take note: The corporate conservatives and their allies in the political and Religious Right are achieving a vast transformation of American life that only they understand because they are its advocates, its architects, and its beneficiaries. In creating the greatest economic inequality in the advanced world, they have saddled our nation, our states, and our cities and counties with structural deficits that will last until our children's children are ready for retirement; and they are systematically stripping government of all its functions except rewarding the rich and waging war.

And, yes, they are proud of what they have done to our economy and our society. If instead of producing a news magazine I was writing for *Saturday Night Live,* I couldn't have made up the things that this crew in Washington have been saying. The president's chief economic adviser says shipping technical and professional jobs overseas is good for the economy. The president's Council of Economic Advisers reports that hamburger chefs in fast food restaurants can be considered manufacturing workers. The president's labor secretary says it doesn't matter if job growth has stalled because "the stock market is the ultimate arbiter." And the president's Federal Reserve chair says that the tax cuts may force cutbacks in Social Security — but hey, we should make the tax cuts permanent anyway.

You just can't make this stuff up. You have to hear it to believe it. This may be the first class war in history where the victims will die laughing.

But what they are doing to middle class and working Americans and the poor — and to the workings of American democracy — is no laughing matter. It calls for righteous indignation and action. Otherwise our democracy will degenerate into a shell of itself in which the privileged and the powerful sustain their own way of life at the expense of others and the United States becomes another Latin America with a small crust of the rich at the top governing a nation of serfs.

Bill Moyers

Over the past few years, as the poor got poorer, the health care crisis worsened, wealth and media became more and more concentrated, and our political system was bought out from under us, prophetic Christianity lost its voice. The Religious Right drowned everyone else out.

And they hijacked Jesus. The very Jesus who stood in Nazareth and proclaimed, "The Lord has anointed me to preach the good news to the poor." The very Jesus who told 5,000 hungry people that all of you will be fed, not just some of you. The very Jesus who challenged the religious orthodoxy of the day by feeding the hungry on the Sabbath, who offered kindness to the prostitute and hospitality to the outcast, who raised the status of women and treated even the tax collector like a child of God. The very Jesus who drove the money changers from the temple. This Jesus has been hijacked and turned into a guardian of privilege instead of a champion of the dispossessed. Hijacked, he was made over into a militarist, hedonist, and lobbyist, sent prowling the halls of Congress in Guccis, seeking tax breaks and loopholes for the powerful, costly new weapon systems that don't work, and punitive public policies.

Let's get Jesus back. The Jesus who inspired a Methodist ship-caulker named Edward Rogers to crusade across New England for an eight-hour work day. Let's get back the Jesus who caused Frances William to rise up against the sweatshop. The Jesus who called a young priest named John Ryan to champion child labor laws, unemployment insurance, a minimum wage, and decent housing for the poor — 10 years before the New Deal. The Jesus in whose name Dorothy Day challenged the church to march alongside auto workers in Michigan, fishermen and textile workers in Massachusetts, brewery workers in New York, and marble cutters in Vermont. The Jesus who led Martin Luther King to Memphis to join sanitation workers in their struggle for a decent wage.

That Jesus has been scourged by his own followers, dragged through the streets by pious crowds, and crucified on a cross of privilege. Mel Gibson missed that. He missed the resurrection —

the spiritual awakening that followed the death of Jesus. He missed Pentecost.

Our times cry out for a new politics of justice. This is no partisan issue. It doesn't matter if you're a liberal or a conservative, Jesus is both and neither. It doesn't matter if you're a Democrat or Republican, Jesus is both and neither. We need a faith that takes on the corruption of both parties. We need a faith that challenges complacency of all power. If you're a Democrat, shake them up. If you're a Republican, shame them. Jesus drove the money changers from the temple. We must drive them from the temples of democracy. Let's get Jesus back.

But let's do it in love. I know it can sound banal and facile to say this. The word "love" gets thrown around too casually these days. And brute reality can mock the whole idea of loving one another. We're still living in the shadow of Dachau and Buchenwald. The smoke still rises above Kosovo and Rwanda, Chechnya and East Timor. The walls of Abu Ghraib still shriek of pain. What has love done? Where is there any real milk of human kindness?

But the love I mean is the love described by Reinhold Niebuhr in his book of essays *Justice and Mercy,* where he writes: "When we talk about love we have to become mature or we will become sentimental. Basically love means... being responsible, responsibility to our family, toward our civilization, and now by the pressures of history, toward the universe of humankind."

What I'm talking about will be hard, devoid of sentiment and practical as nails. But love is action, not sentiment. When the church was young and fair, and people passed by her doors, they did not comment on the difference or the doctrines. Those stern and taciturn pagans said of the Christians: "How they love one another!" It started that way soon after the death of Jesus. His disciple Peter said to the first churches, "Above all things, have unfailing love toward one another." I looked in my old Greek concordance the other day. That word "unfailing" would be more accurately rendered "intense."

Glenn Tinder reminds us that none are good but all are sacred. I want to think this is what the founders meant when they included the not-so-self-evident assertion that "all men are created equal." Truly life is not fair and it is never equal. But I believe the founders were speaking a powerful spiritual truth that is the heart of our hope for this country. They saw America as a great promise — and it is.

But America is a broken promise, and we are called to do what we can to fix it — to get America back on the track. St. Augustine shows us how: "One loving soul sets another on fire." But to move beyond sentimentality, what begins in love must lead on to justice. We are called to the fight of our lives.

Bill Moyers, host of PBS's *Now with Bill Moyers,* has received more than thirty Emmy Awards for excellence in broadcast journalism. Moyers was senior news analyst for the CBS Evening News and Special Assistant to President Lyndon B. Johnson. He holds a Master of Divinity degree from Southwestern Baptist Theological Seminary. This article is adapted from Moyers's keynote address at Call to Renewal's Pentecost 2004 conference in May in Washington, D.C.

4

7 Habits of Highly Effective Mass-Goers

David Philippart

The secret to getting the most out of Mass may be easier than you think. Try these seven simple steps that allow the Mass to do its work on you.

Have you ever tried to have a conversation with someone who won't respond? Or tried to dance with someone who won't move? What would happen if the outfielders just stood there and stared as the ball was hit deep into center?

In all of these situations, the participation of each person is necessary for the event to be successful. We admit the outfielder that won't run and catch has little right to complain about the score. You can't complain if you didn't try. And the better you become at the task, the greater your satisfaction.

Believe it or not, this is true of liturgy, too. In one sense, you take from the liturgy what you put into it. (In another sense, all the good that comes from the liturgy is a pure gift from God.) When you participate in the liturgy fully, consciously, and actively, you benefit more from it.

Sure, sometimes you'll be bored. Sometimes you'll just go through the motions — that's human nature. And it's not a problem when it's occasional. But if you strive to participate, most of the time your

---

Reprinted from *U.S. Catholic*.

mind, heart, and body will be caught up in our great act of thanks and praise.

This is true even when the liturgy is not enacted with care. Even if the music is out of tune and poorly accompanied, even if the prayers and readings are delivered as though being read for the first time, even if the homily is inane, it's still possible to leave the celebration nourished and on fire. We may not be able to control how the liturgy is done in our parish — although we should speak up if it is not being celebrated with care — but we can control whether or not we listen with our hearts and sing our parts with gusto.

The good news is this: While we need to cooperate with Christ in celebrating the liturgy, the power of the Mass does not depend on us. Christ always and perfectly does his part. We need only to open ourselves up to him and the Mass will "work."

"Lift up your hearts!" the priest bids us at the very heart of the Mass itself. That's the challenge: Put your heart into this. Liturgy is a divine-human affair. God always fulfills the "divine" part of the bargain. So how might we participate better at Mass?

1. Enter into Mystery

The Greek word for church means "those whom God has called together." Adopted by God in Baptism, we are brothers and sisters of Christ and hence brothers and sisters of each other. No other bond, not age or race or ethnicity or sexual orientation or political affiliation or economic status or educational background — not even biological relationship — is stronger than the bond of the water of Baptism that draws us together. This water is thicker than blood. This does not mean we all have to be best friends. But we have to act like we are more than just a bunch of strangers in the same room at the same time doing the same thing.

Try this: Be aware of others as you get out of your car or walk toward your church. Make eye contact. Smile, nod, say hello. Remember that after he rose from the dead, Christ appeared to the two disciples on the road to Emmaus as a stranger. And Mary Magdalene mistook him for the gardener.

Consider arriving early so you can spend some time in quiet solitude in the Blessed Sacrament chapel if your church has one. The Eucharist reserved in the tabernacle came from a prior celebration of the Mass, so praying in the presence of Christ in this manner can help us meditate on how to enter more deeply into the sacrifice the next time we go to Mass.

Bless yourself with holy water to remember who you are (a baptized person) and why you are here (because you are a baptized person). If you see the gifts of bread and wine set out, stop for a minute. Look at the bread. Place alongside the bread all that you accomplished in the past week: the work you did, the test you took, all the simple acts of kindness you performed. Also place there all the things the parish did this past week to educate children, care for the sick, feed the hungry, stand up for the oppressed.

Look at the flagon of wine. Put into the flagon all the struggles that you undertook in the past week: to understand others better, to love others more. Put in the flagon, too, all the things the parish struggles with: the attempts to be a more inclusive community, a more vibrant community, a more faithful community. These, then, are the things we will offer to God under the signs of bread and wine.

Take a seat up front and move to the center. This isn't being proud. Save the seats by the doors for those who arrive late. Save the seats on the aisles for those who may have to exercise a ministry, walk a baby, or sit next to someone in a wheelchair.

Bow to the altar before taking your place. Don't just nod your head: Bend deeply, gracefully from the waist. Recognize Christ in this sign: a dining table where God eats with us and heaven comes to earth like a feast comes to those who are starving. When you bow to the altar, you bow to Christ.

If the tabernacle is not in its own chapel but in the main body of the church, our tradition is to genuflect to the tabernacle instead of bowing to the altar. After acknowledging Christ present at the altar or in the tabernacle, acknowledge Christ present in those sitting around you. Say hello, or at least offer a simple smile and a nod. Some people like to kneel and pray after taking their seat. In some monasteries, the practice is to stand attentively for a few moments before sitting. When you sit, prepare your donation and find the opening song. If you picked up the bulletin, don't read it now.

2. Sing for Your Supper

Singing together blends many voices into one. Won't you join your voice to the great voice of the Body of Christ? The musicians are there to lead and to help, not to perform. We are there not to be entertained, but to sing.

Singing together is a great experience. Assembling as the church at liturgy gives us an opportunity rarely found in our technological culture: an opportunity to make music with our voices, to sing together. There is a power in our common song to spread joy to hearts that are without joy, to share sorrow so that the burden is lighter for all, to give voice to hope and yearning and gratitude and love that words alone cannot express.

3. Listen: It's Hard Work

It's hard to simply listen today. We are so used to seeing a story as well as hearing it: watching television, going to the movies. And it's hard enough to follow the plot of a contemporary soap opera, let alone the stories of ancient Israel and the first Christians. But Baptism gives us the grace to hear the Word of God. Just as Jesus opened the ears of the man who could not hear, he opens our ears to hear God speaking to us today in the old and holy words of scripture.

Think of the times a loved one tried to tell you something you didn't quite understand at first. What did you do? You probably positioned your body carefully so you could pay attention. You listened hard, with your heart and mind as well as your ears.

The proclaiming of scripture and preaching at Mass is like this. The One who loves us beyond all telling is telling us. The proclaiming of scripture and the preaching of the homily at Mass is not like someone giving a report, it is a living dialogue between God and the church. And when God speaks, things happen.

So strive to listen. Position your body so that you can concentrate. Unless you have a hearing impairment or difficulty understanding the language in which the scriptures are read, put down the missal and truly listen. When we have a lively dialogue with someone we love, we don't read the newspaper at the same time. We look into each other's eyes and listen deeply. We should do the same thing with the reader and the preacher.

Not every homily will be engaging. Some will even be horrible. If the preaching is consistently terrible, we need to speak up. Charitably, we need to make some positive suggestions to help the priest or deacon do better. Offer to be part of a homily preparation group that meets early in the week to allow those who preach to pray together, share insights into the scripture, even practice and be critiqued. But remember that even in the worst homily, God may still be trying to tell us something. Listen for that, and try to disregard the rest. Don't worry about understanding every word. Let the scripture and homily wash over you, and pay attention to the droplets that stick.

Some people read the assigned scriptures before Mass. The citations are often in the bulletin, or the readings themselves can be found online at *www.usccb.org/nab/index.htm*. Most people, though, can't always make such preparation. So try this: Return to the scriptures that were read first at Mass again and again throughout the week. If nothing else, try to remember the verse from the responsorial psalm and use it as your prayer during the week.

During periods of silence, don't pick the lint off your lapel, futz with or read anything. Listen for God's voice. If you listen hard, you'll hear it.

4. Be a Beggar

After the homily, the general intercessions — or prayers of the faithful — often slip by us. Too bad, because what could happen here is powerful. As baptized people, we share in Christ's priesthood. Part of what a priest does is to ask God to care for those in need, especially those who can't ask for themselves.

The general intercessions are our opportunity to beg God for help. Not because God needs to be persuaded to lend a hand. It's more like this: When we hear a cry for help in the world and bring it to the liturgy, we begin to generate in ourselves and in our community the energy and momentum of compassion. And we know that if we are going to dare to ask God for help in this matter, we had better stand ready to be part of God's answer to our prayer. So by praying these general intercessions, we begin the long and hard work of bearing one another's burdens. The early church took this so seriously that only the baptized were allowed in the room when the prayers of the faithful were prayed.

5. Give It Up!

When we come to the heart of the Mass — the great prayer of thanks and praise — put your heart into it! After you make your donation, stop for a second and think of all the things you are most thankful for right now. As you watch the gifts of bread and wine being placed on the altar, remember that you put yourself alongside that bread and in that flagon when you first came in. Know that you (and we) are being offered to God under the signs of bread and wine.

And here's the miracle. The God who created the heavens and the earth and everything in them, the God who wove the night sky and buttoned it with stars — the living God accepts our gift of self under the sign of bread and wine. Then God changes those gifts into the Body and the Blood of his beloved child Jesus Christ and gives it back to us.

Our medieval ancestors wanted to know precisely at what point the bread and wine become Christ's Body and Blood. They settled on Christ's very own words that the priest repeats in the middle of the Eucharistic Prayer, and these words came to be called "the consecration." Today we are aware that the whole Eucharistic Prayer consecrates the gifts. It would be a grave mistake for a priest to omit all but the words of consecration. In fact, a few years ago, the pope approved an ancient Eucharistic Prayer for continued use in some of the Eastern churches. It's called the Anaphora of Addai and Mari. It does not contain the words of consecration but in other words calls down the Holy Spirit to make the gifts the Body and the Blood of Christ. The pope said that this prayer still consecrates.

It's easy to check out while the priest says the long Eucharistic Prayer. Don't do it! Don't miss out on the divine gift exchange. Especially important are our acclamations that are part of this prayer: the Holy, Holy; the Memorial Acclamation; and the Great Amen. Sing them from your heart, and remember that in doing so we are joining in the singing of the angels and the saints before God's throne.

Next we pray the Lord's Prayer together, and it's easy to simply recite it from memory without thinking much about it. Here's where posture can help. Our bodies can help keep our minds centered on the meaning of these most beautiful words. If your parish holds hands, then hold hands. But otherwise, try this: Pray the Lord's Prayer standing in the orans position. Stand straight with your arms extended from the elbows, hands open, fingers relaxed, palms facing up. Raise your eyes to heaven, too.

This is an ancient prayer gesture that the priest still uses in the Mass today. But it is not a priests-only gesture. It used to be used by all Christians.

The kiss of peace is probably the most misunderstood part of the Mass. But like the general intercessions, in the early church giving the kiss of Christ's peace was something reserved to those who were baptized. Although in the United States we have changed the kiss to a handshake, there's nothing "how-do-you-do" about this gesture. When two baptized people wish peace to each other, they are imparting to each other the blessing of Christ's peace.

So enter into this gesture knowing that you are giving and receiving Christ's peace. Don't chit-chat. Look the other person in the eye. If you don't embrace, then clasp — but don't shake — hands. Hold the other person's hand in both of yours. Wish him or her peace. Share the peace with those around you. This is a symbolic gesture, so you don't have to reach everybody.

6. Sing, Walk, Eat, Drink

"Going up to Communion" is not meant to be like going through the drive-through at a fast food restaurant. It's a communal procession in which we walk and sing together in order to eat and drink together. The communion that we share is on two levels: our communion with Christ and our communion with each other.

So sing as you walk! Most music ministers now use Communion songs with short refrains so that you won't need to carry a hymnal or song sheet. (If they don't, you might suggest it.) Walk with the music. If you receive Communion in your mouth, walk with hands folded. If you receive Communion in your hand, walk forward with your one hand cupped in the other, palm upward, ready — eager — to receive.

Don't pass by the cup! (Unless of course, you have a very specific medical reason for doing so.) The chances of catching a cold or worse are minuscule. But the chances of catching Christ's life and spirit as well as communion with Christ and your sisters and brothers is high.

If it's your parish's custom to bow before receiving the consecrated bread and the consecrated wine, then do so slowly, deliberately, gracefully.

Sing on your way back to your place. Even though most parishes in the U.S. don't do so, the official posture during Communion is to stand until all have received. But if your parish kneels or sits, then do what you are comfortable doing. Keep singing. This song is not distraction, but one of the methods that Christ uses to make us one with him and with each other.

If you were taught to kneel and bury your face in your hands after Communion, you may want to rethink this practice. It's not that it's bad or wrong, although it is hard to sing this way. Rather, on further reflection, there may be practices that better enable you to participate fully in the Mass at this point. The Mass is not time for private prayer — it is thoroughly a communal act. This may sound harsh, especially since many of us yearn today for moments of solitude.

The Mass, especially at this point, is not about solitude, but about communion, being one with others in Christ.

Try this: While singing the Communion song, watch the faces of others going to and coming back from the altar. See in each face the face of Christ. Remember that after his Resurrection, Jesus often appeared to his followers in the guise of a stranger. But it was in the breaking of the bread that they recognized him.

There should be a period of communal silence after all have received Communion and the singing is completed. Here is our opportunity to "rest in the Lord" for a moment before finishing up and going back into the fray of daily living. Here, you may bow your head and close your eyes if that helps you pray. Whatever posture you assume, don't fidget with your belongings or read the bulletin. Simply say "thanks" to God in the silence of your heart.

7. Go to Do Likewise

Participating fully in the Mass trains us to live more fully outside of church, too. When we recognize Christ present in our neighbor-parishioners, we learn to recognize Christ in all people, especially in the poor. When we train our hearts to listen to God's Word, we become better listeners for those we love. Our ears are better attuned to the cries of the poor.

When we intercede for those who are too downtrodden even to ask for help, we find the strength and wisdom to help them. When we offer ourselves to God with the bread and wine, we learn to be bread for those who hunger and wine for those who thirst. And when we share together in the Lord's supper, when we eat and drink the Body and Blood of Christ — well, you know what they say: You are what you eat.

David Philippart is the editor of *Liturgical Catechesis* magazine.

5

Irshad Manji

Stephen Swecker

Irshad Manji is a journalist, author, TV personality and media entrepreneur based in Toronto. In 1972, she and her family came to Vancouver as refugees from Idi Amin's Uganda. *Ms. Magazine* has named her a "Feminist for the 21st Century," and *The New York Times* has called her "Osama bin Laden's worst nightmare." Oprah Winfrey honored her with the first annual Chutzpah Award for "audacity, nerve, boldness and conviction." Ms. Manji hosts *Big Ideas*, a weekly show aimed at college students featuring thinkers who are changing how we view the world. Ms. Manji is the author of *The Trouble with Islam: A Muslim's Call for Reform in Her Faith* (St. Martin's Press). *Zion's Herald* interviewed Ms. Manji on July 17, 2004, at her home in Toronto.

Zion's Herald: — In your book you describe Islam as being a gift of the Jews. Really?

Irshad Manji: What most people, including most Muslims, don't realize is that Islam comes from the Judeo-Christian tradition. The Koran itself says that it is meant only to restore earlier revelations, mainly the Torah and subsequently the Bible. It is a fact that all the biggies of Islam, as a monotheistic religion, started with Judaism, from the unity of God's creation, the oneness of God, to the notion of everlasting life, to our inherent capacity as human beings to choose good over evil. Even the concept of free will. All of these began with Judaism.

Reprinted from *Zion's Herald*.

ZH: You imply, however, that Islam is perhaps more "narrow-minded." I think you use that phrase.

IM: I do.

ZH: What does that have to do with the current situation in Islam?

IM: The trouble with Islam today is that literalism is fast becoming mainstream. I recognize that every faith has its share of literalists. American Christianity has its fundamentalists, some of whom populate the White House. Jews have their ultra-orthodox and orthodox. Buddhists, for God's sake, have their evangelicals. But only within Islam is literalism fast becoming mainstream. We Muslims, even here in the West, are routinely raised to believe that because the Koran came after the Torah and the Bible, chronologically and historically, it is the final and therefore perfect manifesto of God's will. It is, if I can put it like this, "God 3.0," and none shall come after it. This is a supremacy complex that even mainstream Muslims have toward the Koran. This is dangerous, because when abuse happens under the banner of my faith as it is today, most Muslims have no clue how to debate, dissent, revise or reform. Not because we're stupid, but because we have never been introduced to the possibility, let alone the virtue, of asking questions about our holy book.

ZH: How did Islam get to that point?

IM: Let me explain what Islam once had and then what happened to it. During the golden age of Islam, roughly between the ninth and 11th centuries, the faith embraced a tradition of critical thinking known as ijtihad. Thanks to the spirit of ijtihad, 135 schools of thought flourished during this time. In Muslim Spain, for example, scholars would teach their students to abandon "expert opinion" if the experts' own teachings contradicted the Koran or if the students came up with better evidence for their ideas. Toward the end of the 11th century, however, the gates of ijtihad were deliberately slammed shut.

ZH: Why was that?

IM: For political reasons. During this time the fragile Muslim Empire, spanning from Iraq all the way to Spain, was experiencing a series of internal convulsions. Dissident denominations were popping up and declaring their own runaway governments. So, the main Muslim leader, based in Baghdad, closed ranks politically. He reduced 135 schools of thought to only four schools of thought, and pretty conservative schools of thought at that. This led to a rigid reading of the Koran and to a series of legal opinions that we know as fatwas. Not death warrants, necessarily, but legal opinions that scholars could no longer overturn or even question, but could now on pain of execution only imitate. To this very day, that's what most Muslim scholars have been doing, imitating each other's prejudices without much reflection or self-criticism or introspection. The intellectual heritage of Islam died from that point on.

ZH: Imitation as a mode of transmitting a tradition — might that also be viewed as uncritical obedience to authority — the authority of the past?

IM: You're right. It becomes authoritarianism.

ZH: Yet, as I understand it, Islam has no central or single source of authority other than the Koran. There's no Islam equivalent of the Vatican, for example.

IM: Well, yes and no...as with everything in religion! It's true that there isn't a single identifiable figure that leads the entire Islamic world for doctrinal purposes. But, the clergy and the clerical class in Islam have far more power today, and have had for the last 600 years, than they were ever meant to. You know, in Cairo, Al-Azhar University, which is, for lack of a better analogy, the Harvard of Sunni Islam, regularly issues fatwas, legal opinions, that various Sunni communities around the world then follow. One of the things that needs to happen is for Muslims to recognize that Allah gives us free will. "Let there be no compulsion in religion," the Koran says. The right to independent thinking is the right of every individual within Islam, but that right has been allocated to the clerical class alone. I don't feel that there's any reason for that to happen.

ZH: So your project is to relocate the source of authority for Islam, to take authority from the Koran, in other words, and locate it in the thought process of individuals?

IM: I'm certainly not suggesting that what the Koran says doesn't matter if it doesn't speak to our personal experiences. That really would be smorgasbord Islam. But I would put it this way: I believe that as a Muslim I can live by the Koran quite honestly and quite authentically. But what does it mean to live by the Koran? Well, considering that the Koran, like every holy book, is ripe with contradictions and ambiguities, I choose to emphasize the passages that are pro-pluralism, pro-diversity and pro-freedom of expression.

I'll give you what I think is a pretty reasonable approach to the Koran. For all of its contradictions, there are three consistent messages from the beginning to the middle to the end. The first is that only God knows fully the truth of anything. Second, as a result, only God can punish disbelief. Finally, as a result of our need for humility, since only God knows fully the truth of anything, we Muslims have to be open to the freedom of exploration, and not just for ourselves, but for all people.

ZH: There are a lot of people in the Christian world, particularly Protestant Christians, who would say much the same thing. We refer to it as "radical monotheism," and believe that all life is under the judgment of God.

IM: Right, and there are those who take the point that you made one step further and say, "So, really, how does your Islam differ from Christianity?" My answer would be, "Why does it have to differ?" If, in fact, we can believe the Koran is meant only to restore earlier revelations, then there actually do not need to be major theological differences among the three monotheisms. Doctrinal and ritualistic differences, sure, but major spiritual differences? I'm not so insecure as a Muslim that I need to cling to what Sigmund Freud would call "the narcissism of small differences."

ZH: Following on that, let me ask you a rather personal question. How did you, Irshad, a Muslim woman, mature into what strikes me as such a healthy, self-assured approach to life?

IM: I'm sure I'm a far more complex psychiatric case than even I want to think about! But I can tell you what one of the most significant influences on my life has been — the refugee experience. I came to North America as a refugee, along with my family. Even as a child, although I wasn't able to articulate it in quite this way, I knew I was incredibly fortunate to be living in a society where, as a Muslim woman, I can be engaged, and I don't just mean for marriage — where I could dream big dreams and tap much of my potential. Instinctively, I understood the difference between living in a closed society and living in an open society. To this day, I carry that love of my democratic freedoms with me because I know what a closed society looks and feels like, and I can tell you, it sucks!

ZH: You apparently had what one might call a worldview shift very early in your life, one that has taken hold in you very deeply....

IM: I would go one better. Growing up in this part of the world actually has saved my faith in my faith. I know that's counter-intuitive, especially at a time when it's easy to accept the premise that the West is the enemy of Islam. It's quite the opposite for me. It's because of the freedoms to research, examine and exchange ideas, and to challenge and be challenged, that I learned about the progressive side of my religion, mainly the spirit of ijtihad. I never would have learned that had I remained in that insular Muslim microcosm known as the madressa.

ZH: But aren't most Muslims still in the madressa, so to speak? How in the world is the personal reformation that you've experienced because you happened to come to Canada as a child — how likely is it to happen for the billion other Muslims who won't have a chance to do what you've done?

IM: I wish I could tell you I have the magic answer. I don't. But I do have some thoughts on how to get the process going. Let me also say right away that I don't think the point here is to clone a bunch of Irshad Manjis. Many would argue, perhaps including my own mother, that one is enough! I think there are two prongs here. One, as you rightly imply, are Muslims in the West. They are best positioned to revive the tradition of ijtihad. We already enjoy the precious freedoms of which I spoke. Now, I don't deny that Muslims in the West are also targets of harassment, profiling and discrimination. I've experienced it myself. But these do not compare to what millions upon millions of other Muslims elsewhere are going through at the hands of fellow Muslims.

Our freedom in the West is a precious gift, and my challenge to my fellow Muslims is, what in God's name are we doing with that gift? However, even if the liberal reformation begins here, God knows it doesn't end here. So that's the second prong: People throughout the Islamic world, women in particular, need to learn of their right to think for themselves. In my book I outline a global campaign to promote innovative approaches to Islam that I call "Operation Ijtihad."

ZH: Well, you answered my question, but I still wonder about the mechanics.

IM: That's right. The devil truly is in the details in this case.

ZH: So, would you regard your book as an agenda for your generation of Muslims?

IM: There's prescience in your question because when you talk about my generation, I can affirm for you that one of the most responsive groups of Muslims from whom I'm hearing are young Muslims. No question I'm hearing anger and vitriol, too. Every few days a very concrete death threat comes through my website. From time to time I even get death threats in places like airports. That is not the surprising part. I fully expected it. The most surprising aspect of my life since the release of my book has been the positive response from Muslims around the world, not just the West, and two groups in particular: Muslim women and young Muslims.

ZH: I want to ask you about the relationship between homosexuality and spirituality. As an openly gay woman, how do you reconcile your sexuality with your religious tradition, which adamantly condemns homosexuality?

IM: I think the first thing for me to emphasize is that being openly gay need not mean being arrogantly gay. In other words, I fully accept the possibility — the possibility — that my Creator rejects my same-sex relationship. As a monotheist, I say that only God can make that judgment. In the meantime, I have a lot of reconciling to do, but those who argue that Islam and homosexuality cannot be reconciled have their own reconciling to do. Let me give you an example. You know, the Koran is really explicit that everything God created is "excellent." Further, nothing that God created is "in vain" and God creates "whom He will." How, then, do my detractors reconcile those statements with their utter condemnation of homosexuality? Again, I'm not saying I'm right. I may not be. But I am challenging my detractors to tell me why they know, not just believe, but why they know they are so right. What I am asking my fellow Muslims to tolerate is not my sexual orientation. I don't seek their approval. They didn't create me nor will they undo me. What I am asking of my fellow Muslims is a willingness to debate these issues rather than take them as a given, to tolerate the fact that there is ambiguity in all of this.

If, in fact, we can believe the Koran is meant only to restore earlier revelations, then there actually do not need to be major theological differences among the three monotheisms.

ZH: Your perspective, if taken seriously, could open lots of doors to conversation, and not just among Muslims.

IM: For what it's worth, I began advocating for religious reform long before I knew what sexual orientation I was. So, I truly do not think that my being a lesbian, out or not, has influenced in a radical way my willingness to dissent with the mainstream. I think that I would have dissented whether I was straight, gay or celibate. There are bigger moral issues that have led me to this point. Not the least of which, of course, is the anti-Semitism that runs so rampant within the faith today.

ZH: You might surprise some people in the West about your convictions regarding the Israeli-Palestinian conflict. What would you say about that?

IM: I would call it a pretty moderate position. I view the conflict as shared culpability. I'm pro-Palestine in the sense that I, like so many people, want an independent state for the Palestinian people.

But what I will not do is let the Palestinian leadership off the hook for its role in how we've come to be where we are. There have been many attempts to grant the Palestinian people an independent state. But the Palestinian leadership has rejected each and every proposal. What is more galling to me as a democrat, a small d democrat, is that at no time has the Palestinian leadership ever consulted the people themselves about whether these proposals ought to be accepted or rejected. A little known fact: the Oslo Peace Agreement was never translated into Arabic so the people could read it for themselves. There actually are two occupations going on. One is the military occupation, which I cannot deny exists. But the other is the political or ideological occupation of the Palestinian people, and that can be laid at the feet of their so-called leaders. Both have to be cleaned up in order for a sustainable peace to take place.

ZH: In your book you described a revelatory moment when you were near the Western Wall in Jerusalem.

IM: I told the story about an Orthodox Jewish kid with his prayer shawl hanging out of his baggy pants and his curls dangling down from his temples. He was racing around on one of those sleek silver scooters, and I'm turning the corner into the old Jewish quarter of Jerusalem on my way to the Western Wall when he runs into me. At that moment, I thought to myself, you know, here is a child who lives what many would call an ultra-insular life in a quarter of one of the world's oldest cities and one of the oldest quarters of that city, and he probably goes to a yeshiva and is taught all kinds of do's and don'ts — mostly don'ts. And yet, here he has the freedom to race around on a consumer vehicle, obviously imported from somewhere in North America, and nothing stops him from identifying himself as a fun-loving free spirit. It occurred to me at that moment that if ultra-Orthodox Jews can give themselves that kind of freedom, what is stopping moderate Muslims from doing the same? We, too, percolate with paradoxes. It's actually OK to struggle to reconcile those paradoxes. I saw something in motion about that child, and I don't just mean the scooter, but the spirit of exuberance. I don't see that in a lot of Muslim kids. It's the crushing of that spirit that I am most troubled by.

ZH: On an unrelated matter, have you seen *Fahrenheit 9/11*? What is your take on it?

IM: My take on it is my take on Michael Moore. The world needs polemicists. Some would argue I'm one, too. But Moore routinely employs a tactic that I try to avoid. It's the tactic of, "My fundamentalism is better than your fundamentalism." I believe that fundamentalism of any stripe — cultural, religious, sexual, whatever — reduces each of us to something less than our multi-faceted self. It reduces issues to something less than their multi-faceted natures. I would hope, therefore, that in the kind of polemic that I write that I bring not just a degree of hope but a certain degree of reason and a respect for the grand audience that is out there. Life is much more complex because the Creator is much more complex than any of our tidy theories about life.

Stephen Swecker is the editor of *The Progressive Christian* magazine.

6

The Lonely Road of Matty Wilson

David Wilson

Some highways have souls; others are merely pavement. The soul of Highway 16, the 720-km-long branch of the Trans-Canada that spans northern British Columbia from Prince George to Prince Rupert, is deeply troubled.

It's a mean road. Logging trucks, as rickety as they are over-laden, roar its length day and night. Convoys of motor homes labor up the long mountain passes, as if to taunt other drivers to acts of stunning recklessness. Further east, toward Prince George, the landscape flattens and the highway stretches mournfully to the horizon; the mind grows dim and the foot heavy.

Small roadside shrines — a wooden cross and maybe a withered wreath or some plastic flowers — mark the places where death has visited Highway 16. Sometimes you can still see the skid marks that map someone's final seconds. Drive long enough and you learn to spot these places before you get there: a sharp turn in the distance; a logging road up ahead; a pull-off at the crest of a hill.

These dangers you can see. What you can't see is the highway's terrible secret. Since 1990, six young women have been victims of foul play along Highway 16. Three were eventually found murdered, while three vanished without a trace and are presumed dead. None of the cases has been solved.

Reprinted from *The United Church Observer*.

The first five victims were Aboriginal.

Fifteen-year-old Delphine Nikal disappeared in June 1990 as she hitchhiked east from her hometown of Smithers. Four more Native women in their teens — Ramona Wilson, 15, Roxanne Thiara, 15, Alishia Germaine, 15 and Lana Derrick, 19 — met with grief during a 16-month stretch starting in June 1994.

While police say there's nothing to link the cases, many in northern B.C. believe a serial killer is at large. (Privately some say they hope it's a serial killer: better one killer than six.)

Like the missing women of Vancouver's Downtown East Side before the arrest of Robert Pickton, the stories of the missing and murdered Aboriginal women of Highway 16 barely register on the public radar. A national campaign launched last spring by the Native Women's Association of Canada (NWAC) and supported by the United Church hopes to change that. It's called Sisters in Spirit, and it urges the federal government to set up a multi-million-dollar fund to research and document hundreds of missing or murdered Native women. Highway 16 is a prime focus, not only for the cases that are known, but also for suggestions that many more have gone unreported because families don't trust the justice system.

The best-known missing-woman case on Highway 16 is the most recent. On a June afternoon two years ago, friends drove 25-year-old Nicole Hoar to a popular hitchhiking jump-off on the outskirts of Prince George. A summer tree-planter, Nicole told co-workers she was heading 370 km west to Smithers to pay a surprise visit to her sister and attend a music festival during a week off. She spoke to at least one prospective ride — a man with children who wasn't driving as far as she wanted to go — before vanishing. She is the lone white woman among the missing women of Highway 16.

Nicole's employer reported her missing six days after she was supposed to have returned to work. Police and volunteers mounted a huge search effort believed to be the largest ever in northern B.C. A dozen RCMP officers and 170 volunteers scoured a 24,000-square-km area between Prince George and Smithers, knocking on doors and covering 8,000 km of roadway, ditches, logging roads, hiking trails and campsites. Helicopters and fixed-wing aircraft searched from above.

After four days the official search was called off. But the huge outpouring of support for the young woman and her family back in Red Deer, Alta., continued for weeks afterwards. Police sifted through more than 1,400 tips. A reward fund grew to $25,000, then $35,000. Art exhibitions and concerts — even an attempt to set a speedskating world record by friend and 2002 Olympian Steven Elm — were held in Nicole's benefit. A Web site, *www.findnicolehoar.com*, still operates.

Two years later Nicole's disappearance remains unsolved. The intense media coverage has died down, but you still see signs of those terrible, panic- and grief-filled days in the early summer of 2002. Reward posters with pictures of Nicole and details of her disappearance hang in gas stations, diners and general stores up and down Highway 16.

They're a reminder of the highway's sinister side. Highway 16 passes through some breathtaking wilderness, but knowing what has happened here deforms the landscape. As you drive the long, lonely blacktop, your thoughts begin to drift where they shouldn't: Did a killer pull into this rest-stop? Did the victim see the sunlight glinting off that lake? What must she have been thinking?

Dangerous questions for a dangerous road. You begin to understand why they sometimes call this the Highway of Tears. But then you hear Matilda Wilson's story and realize you have no idea what tears really are.

Matty Wilson laughs easily, but her laugh has a way of trailing off into a care-worn sigh. She divides her time between her house in Smithers and working as a cook in logging camps. The first thing I noticed when I walked into her house last summer was a small table near the doorway and some pictures on the wall of a pretty teenaged girl with long, straight dark hair. Ramona.

Matty Wilson is Gitxsan, a residential school survivor, born in Hazelton, B.C., 54 years ago. In 1994, she was a single mother of six living in the Aboriginal neighborhood along Railway Ave. in Smithers. Her oldest child, Brenda, was 28. Ramona was her youngest, 15 and in Grade 9.

Ramona was very much the baby of the family, says Brenda, doted on by her older siblings and pampered by her mother. Matty loved to brush Ramona's long, thick hair and made sure she always dressed well. The attention seemed to be paying off: Matty's "kind, giggly little girl" did fine at school, was good at sports, worked part-time at a pancake house and, in the late spring of 1994, was hired as a part-time peer counselor at a community service agency. The job was tailor-made — she had her sights set on a career as a psychologist.

Matty says she was surprised but not overly concerned when Ramona failed to show up for her first day on the counseling job. It was June and end-of-school parties were everywhere. Kids often stayed out late, thumbed rides from party to party and slept over at friends'.

But Ramona wasn't with her friends. She'd been seen in downtown Smithers at mid-day on June 11, but not since. Some speculated she'd set out to meet her boyfriend in Moricetown, a Wet'su-wet'en village about 35 km west on Highway 16. But no one there had seen her. At first, police leaned to the view that she had run away. When her birth control pills and an uncashed paycheck were found in her room at home, everyone began to suspect something more serious.

For Matty the first few days were a vortex of fear and confusion. Police had "not much to go on," she says. She and her children needed to do something but had no idea what. "We were on our own, stumbling in the dark," says Brenda. Her brothers and a few friends searched in and around town while Matty and Brenda worked the phones.

"I never searched," Brenda says, "because I didn't think I could handle it if I found something."

Once-familiar, friendly streets darkened with suspicion. "For the first month, all I did was look at everybody, wondering," says Matty.

Adds Brenda: "I was always aware of how people acted around me, especially if they seemed to be acting nervously."

They searched all that month, then off and on all summer and into the fall. Matty kept in constant touch with the police but it was clear they were making little headway. "They always gave me the same answer: 'We'll contact you if there's anything to report'." By November, police were also searching for 15-year-old Roxanne Thiara, who had gone missing from Prince George. A month later 15-year-old Alishia Germaine's body was discovered behind a Prince George school near the highway. Police told Matty they had their hands full.

Matty's files from that time are a glimpse inside a mother's desperation and mounting isolation. Newspaper items about Ramona are clipped, copied and dated. Notes are jotted in the margins and passages underlined, their significance in some cases known only to Matty. Scraps of paper list the phone numbers of social agencies, radio stations and newspapers. Others bear the home phone numbers of the RCMP officers working the case. A copy of an official "Search Management Registration Assignment Form" lists the clothing and gear needed by search-party members. A photocopy of a missing-person poster is well-thumbed, the words "Ramona Lisa Wilson" underlined in thick black marker.

Notes scribbled on yellow Post-Its and on telephone message slips record Matty's efforts to keep the search for her daughter moving forward:

> "Mary — retrace steps from where she was last seen"
> "Ronda: keep track of rumours"
> "180 tips in his book. Two detectives on the case"
> "Saturday search: wrap up by 5 p.m."
> "Ask Christal about the water tower"
> "Matty: sell tickets to raise money for Ramona's fund"

Money was a problem. Matty didn't have the thousands of dollars needed for reward money. The Gitanmaax First Nation donated

$1,000 to start a reward fund, but Matty knew she needed a lot more than that. Local businesses and industries weren't lining up with offers of help, so Matty decided to raffle off some of her craftwork. First prize was a child's vest; second, a dreamcatcher. Matty and her children set up a table in a local mall and sold tickets at $2 a piece or three for $5. She hoped to raise $9,000 to bring the reward fund to an even $10,000. She came away with $500.

Ramona's birthday in February came and went with no breaks in the case. A psychic tried to help but came up empty. "It was a very, very difficult time for my mother," says Brenda.

Matty continued to believe that a big reward was crucial. With the help of supporters from the local Native friendship centre she organized a fund-raising dance in the parish hall at St. Joseph's Roman Catholic Church, where she worships. Despite her personal anguish she tried to make the event as festive as possible.

It flopped.

Another Smithers fund-raiser that spring was a big success. Merchants, industries and everyday citizens rallied around the town's contribution to a series of events held in memory of Melanie Carpenter, a Surrey, B.C., woman who had been abducted, raped and murdered three months earlier.

The Smithers newspaper, *The Interior News,* was outraged. The paper had been one of Matty's few steadfast supporters, offering free advertising space and ongoing news coverage. "Why did Matilda not benefit from the generosity of our corporate citizens in her campaign to find her daughter?" the paper asked in an editorial. "It took the brutal rape and murder of an unknown in the Lower Mainland before the community of Smithers was called into action. Was it because Melanie Carpenter was white?"

Bitterness still lingers. Jenny Poirier, a worker at the Friendship Centre and a friend of the Wilson family, helped Matty organize her fund-raiser. Her expression grows fierce as she remembers: "I thought it was really ignorant, not to show Ramona any support, but then to show all that support for someone not from here."

Matty finally got the reward money she needed through the Calgary-based Missing Children's Society of Canada. Posters offering $10,000 for information leading to Ramona's whereabouts were released on April 8, 1995, almost 10 months after she disappeared.

Forty-eight hours later, two boys riding on an all-terrain vehicle near the Smithers airport got stuck in the spring mud. They went into the bush to find a log to pry the vehicle free and stumbled upon human remains underneath a tree. Police brought Matty out to the site off Yellich Road. The remains were badly decomposed but there was no mistaking the long, dark hair. It was Ramona.

Ten years later, only one person knows where Ramona Wilson was killed, when she died and how she died. That person remains at large. Why she died is a question as troubling as Highway 16 is long.

Matty Wilson's obsession with finding her daughter has become an obsession with finding her daughter's killer. The 10 months Ramona's body lay in the woods made the RCMP's forensic work all but hopeless. Yet Matty continued to press police when she heard rumors or thought of a fresh angle. She still grasps hopefully at every shred of new information.

Investigators have come and gone. "Every time it's like you have to start over," she says. "There have been a few who have been really interested in the case and tried to get as much information as they can, but they say they don't have much to go on."

Matty and her surviving children hold a public memorial on the anniversary of Ramona's disappearance, and sometimes on her birthday too. "We hope that whoever did this will see that we're not going to give up, no matter how long it takes," says Brenda. Joined by friends and supporters, they gather at the place in the woods where Ramona's body was found or at the intersection of Yellich Road and Highway 16. Sometimes they march along the highway and motorists honk to show their support.

"There are times when I think, 'Oh, what's the use,'" says Brenda. "But then it all comes back and I realize that if we don't do something it could happen again — and it could be a family member or a friend."

Matty also talks to the media. "It's very painful," she says, "but it's the only way I can keep it going."

When Nicole Hoar vanished two years ago, media interest in the missing and murdered women of Highway 16 suddenly surged. Reporters came calling for reaction from Matty. "I told them I knew what [Nicole's family] must be going through, and I gave my condolences." Privately, Matty and her children were "devastated" — they have been every time a young woman has gone missing. "We call each other and cry, because we know how it feels." Matty couldn't help but notice the scale of the search effort and the huge outpouring of support for Nicole. She believes the response was appropriate. She also believes it would have been appropriate in Ramona's case.

Matty's public profile is the exception, not the rule. Most families of missing women have chosen to stay private. Frances Stanley led the First Nations Women's Council in Terrace, 220 km west of Smithers during the 1990s. Now a court worker, Stanley was a driving force behind vigils and potluck dinners organized in support of the missing women, notably Lana Derrick, who vanished from Terrace in October 1995. Stanley says cultural traditions run deep and strong in some Aboriginal families: death is a passage, and the private rituals that attend it must be respected. "We are always mindful of our rites of passage, of what we can and can't do," she says. Stanley adds: "It makes it a little difficult to advocate for the missing women."

Some families just want to move on. "There's a fear of revisiting the pain and trauma," says Kathy Wesley-Scott, a member of the Tsimshian First Nation who works as a family violence and sexual abuse counselor in Terrace. That fear often projects right across the Aboriginal community. "People may have dealt with it individually, but they're not well-organized. There's definitely a sense of resistance to the issue in the community, a sense of helplessness."

That sense only heightens the lingering fear that a serial killer roams Highway 16. Lynne Terbasket hosts a public-affairs program on Terrace's Native-run radio station. She has reported on the missing women and has taken part in searches and vigils. "The fear that someone is out there, targeting Aboriginal women, grows every time another woman goes missing," she says.

RCMP special investigators, aided by FBI criminologists and psychological profilers, have concluded there's little to link the disappearances beyond the fact that most of the victims are Aboriginal and were engaged in risky behavior, ranging from hitchhiking to running away to prostitution. The files remain open, and despite officers coming and going, the cases are "constantly being reviewed, and new tips are investigated as they come in," says Staff Sgt. Larry Flath of the RCMP's major crimes unit in Prince George, himself new to the job.

Still, many in the Aboriginal population believe the police and the public are jaundiced when it comes to missing Native women. They saw a stark double standard in the response to the disappearance of Nicole Hoar. It didn't help to read comments like these from an RCMP investigator on the case, speaking to a *Calgary Sun* reporter: "[Nicole] falls outside the mould of so many other disappearances.... Nicole is a university-educated 25-year-old Caucasian woman who has had not so much as a parking ticket."

"The inequalities are clear," says Frances Stanley. "Virtually nothing has been done for the First Nations women who went missing."

"I don't think the Native women are as important in the eyes of the public," says Terbasket, who views the issue as rooted in systemic racism, plain and simple. "Aboriginal women are at risk from the day they're born. You walk around with all this baggage before you can even talk. You've got economic baggage, social baggage, you've got gender baggage." All these factors merge when an Aboriginal woman walks out to Highway 16 and thumbs a ride to the doctor's or to go shopping or to visit family or friends. Of course it's risky, says Terbasket, "but they have no choice. They live in poverty."

It takes courage to be as public as Matty Wilson is about her loss. Her courage has been hard-earned, one tear at a time.

She hasn't always been strong. "My mom has been through some very dark times," says Brenda. Matty flirted with suicide and suffered a mild stroke. For a few years she hid from Ramona's death. "I didn't know where I was," Matty says. She stopped the public memorials because they were more than she could handle.

"When my mom finally realized we were all falling apart too," says Brenda, "that we still needed her even though we were grown up, she came around."

Today, Matty focuses on keeping strong. Grief counseling has helped, and so has her faith. She attends St. Joseph's Roman Catholic Church regularly. "Even if I don't go, I pray on Sundays," she says.

The annual memorials have resumed. They take every ounce of strength Matty has, sometimes more. "In public she holds up pretty good," says family friend Jenny Poirier. "Behind closed doors...."

"It's hard to talk about it," Matty admits. "But it gives me more strength in the long-run. You have to survive, but it's a hard road and I'm still traveling through it."

I first met Matty on warm Wednesday afternoon. After a long talk we agreed to meet the following morning; she would take me to the place where Ramona's body was discovered.

She was a little worse for wear when I picked her up. She said that talking about Ramona is always harder than she thinks it will be.

We drove into Smithers to pick up her son Tim, "to support me," Matty said. Tim was hanging out with his friend Albert Nikal. Albert is the brother of Delphine Nikal, the first of the Highway 16's missing women.

The two men sat silently in the back seat as we drove out of town toward Yellich Road. Matty's conversation was full of must-have's: Ramona's killer must have known his way; he must have been local; he must have driven a pickup.

We turned onto Yellich Road and drove a couple of kilometers, stopping when we reached an open field past the end of the runway at Smithers Airport. We piled out of the car and walked alongside a wooded area.

Tim and Albert led the way. As they turned to enter the woods, a golden eagle swooped out of some low branches and shrieked. Matty called out to Tim. "Did you see that? I wonder what it's trying to say."

The woods were cool and dark. Matty and I picked our way through the underbrush and caught up with Tim and Albert. They were standing beside a balsam tree. Under its sloping boughs, at the base of the trunk, was a flower pot and some plastic flowers.

Matty showed where Ramona's body lay when it was found, where her head had been, how her sneakers were gone. Then she leaned against the tree trunk and exploded in grief.

She sobbed until she was bent double; the forest echoed with her keening. Then Tim said quietly, "Let's go."

Matty crossed herself, straightened up and began to walk away unsteadily. Somewhere up above, the eagle shrieked again.

Matty said, "I wonder what this is all about." She thought for a moment and answered herself. "Maybe it wants some answers."

Then the eagle was gone. All was silent in the woods, except for the distant hum of traffic out on the Highway of Tears.

David Wilson is an associate editor of *The United Church Observer*. David Wilson and Matilda Wilson are not related.

7

A Watch of Love

Instructions for Keeping a Vigil of Life with a Loved One Who Is Dying

Walter Friesen

As I write, my lifelong friend Herb is dying in Juneau, Alaska. I want to be at his side, keeping watch while he lives his death and enters eternal life. I am at peace about what to say and do; I am eager and excited about the vigil, for I know it will be a wonderful deepening of my own spirit.

I cannot be with Herb, but I have sent my words of affection and blessing by email, and Herb's brother Rick has already read them to Herb in the presence of those gathered round, keeping watch.

Most of us feel unsure and unprepared for the vigil of life. We feel drawn to be present, for we do not want our beloved to die alone. But we also feel we are intruding on holy space and wonder whether we have authority to be present and touch, speak, pray, sing, laugh, cry, remember without permission from the one crossing over. It would be the rare exception for the dying to communicate in their final hours the welcome we might seek.

We may feel awkward about who is welcome at the bed in the room. We may feel we cannot be free to speak our hearts because of how it may be understood by others in the room.

And perhaps most difficult, if we haven't talked it through in advance: Does the one dying know she or he is actively dying? Does

---

Reprinted from *The Mennonite*.

the dying one know that we know? Reticence to talk about dying may come from denial by any of us. My experience teaches me that the one dying is rarely in denial but may feel shy and unprepared about speaking of death and may feel constrained to try to comfort the loved ones present by avoiding death topics.

For these reasons it is wisest to talk with our loved ones about death, dying, vigils, wakes, funeral arrangements, burials — and especially wills and advance directives — long before the hour of death. These topics should be discussed regularly and periodically all through life and especially when we score another anniversary or when we move into new living arrangements.

But now we return to the vigil of life, the watch of love at the couch of death. If we have been listening and taking notes, we will have a useful folder that includes important life events with dates, places, people; favorite Bible stories or verses; favorite poems and songs; some photos with a story; some life anecdotes; a bit of humor; words of a wall plaque; references to favorite colors, clothes, expressions, gestures, foods, cars, places. These are all wonderful help for the watch of love.

A time of sharing: If you have invited a health worker or clergy person to be present, you might ask this person to formally open the time of sharing. Or if the family agrees to one of their own to lead the way, that works well. The leader comes near, takes the hand of the dying or gently touches the face and, speaking clearly, firmly says, for example: Mother, this is Walt speaking. We are all here around your bed (name those in the room) to give you our blessings, to sing some songs, to read from the Bible, to tell stories, to pray with you and stay with you as you leave your body and enter into your glory. We all believe that tonight (today) you will finish your life. We all rejoice with you. You have run a good race, you have lived a good life. We are here to tell you good-bye and to send you ahead of us with blessing and joy.

Here one of the group might lead in a prayer or you might recite the Lord's Prayer together — particularly if it was one of your traditions. Or you might sing the Doxology or some other prayer song or praise hymn.

Then, one by one, each person takes the hand of the dying, repeats her or his name and speaks words of love, respect, gratitude, blessing, goodwill and release.

After the first round, if there are important loved ones unable to be present and if there is a message from them (in writing or via telephone) those blessings and releases are also clearly given.

When the first round of blessings and releases is finished, there will be some times of silence and times for hymns, poems, Scriptures and especially memories of events and patterns. (Always try to remember to give your name.)

If any in the group desires a few minutes of private time, that should be arranged. But in general it is good to share your words in each other's presence, for in this way you build and strengthen the bonds of love and respect.

If any knows of events and disappointments in which forgiveness and blessing have not been spoken, it is important to reach a peace-of-heart place in which you can genuinely say: "All my accounts with you are clean. I feel your forgiveness and blessing in my life. You have been a good (mother, son, etc.) to me and I carry your spirit in me. On my side I can assure you that I have and will forgive every wrong or injustice I have ever felt from you. My account with you is all paid up. You may die in peace with me."

Truthfulness: Also, all should be aware that the dying one dearly wishes to know that his or her loved ones will be well, that their futures are open and joyful. If there are personal spiritual-emotional-physical-relational problems that are known to the dying and to the loved ones gathered, it is helpful to acknowledge and name them and to say what you are doing to overcome those trials. It is not perfection that is needed for release but rather honesty. Indeed it is truthfulness that makes us free.

You might talk about your plans and prospects, about your dreams and hopes. These are all life-signs to share. For the dying those thoughts may be comforting.

Do not underestimate the healing in humor and laughter. The vigil does not have to be somber. On the other hand, you may also feel a need for silent waiting, a time of hushed holiness. Let all the moods of life enter naturally.

And you may sense — from prior conversation about the issue or from the spirit of the moment — that your dying loved one may seek to cross over alone with God. Follow your instincts. We know of a number of our loved ones who seemed to wait until we left the room for a few minutes. This dying alone choice does not mean the watch is inappropriate, that the blessings, assurances, releases and memories were not important. It means the final moment is so holy that we want no distraction. This may be especially true for us who have always felt responsible for everyone in our presence.

After the last breath, we may gather round and offer tears and prayers of gratitude and relief. We may linger after the nurse or doctor has come to confirm death. Doctors and nurses may want to join us in prayer and rejoicing. And we may want to linger in the room and start planning the memorial-burial events waiting for the mortician to come.

If pastors have not been present during the vigil but are called at this point, it is helpful for one of the family to be given some consensus authority to take the lead in reporting to the clergy and in working with morticians and clergy on arrangements.

Walter Friesen, Newton, Kansas, is chaplain at Bethesda Home, Goessel, Kansas. This article is adapted from an article in *The Bethesda Letter*.

8

Via Media Groups Unite in Atlanta Meeting

Jan Nunley

Representatives of 12 independent Episcopal groups opposed to efforts to "realign" the Episcopal Church along more conservative lines met together for the first time at a retreat in Atlanta March 25–27, 2004, and emerged as an alliance called Via Media USA.

They represent laypeople and clergy from the grassroots organizations who say they hold diverse opinions about controversial issues in the church, but desire to remain in communion both with the Episcopal Church and the worldwide Anglican Communion. The Via Media groups include Albany Via Media and Concerned Episcopalians of the St. Lawrence Deanery (both in the Diocese of Albany); Episcopal Voices of Central Florida; The Gathering (Dallas); Fort Worth Via Media; Progressive Episcopalians of Pittsburgh (PEP); Via Media Rio Grande (VMRG); E-Way (San Diego); Remain Episcopal (San Joaquin); Episcopal Forum of South Carolina (EFSC); Southwest Florida Via Media Episcopalians; and Springfield Via Media (SVM).

Leaders of the groups said they did not discuss the controversy over the consecration of an openly gay bishop in the Diocese of New Hampshire or the issue of same-sex blessings during their meeting, and preferred not to reveal their individual stances.

"We have acknowledged different perspectives," said the Rev. Michael Russell, rector of All Souls' Episcopal Church in San Diego

---

Reprinted from Episcopal News Service.

and a member of Episcopal Way of San Diego, at the group's closing news conference. "We haven't criticized or judged any of those perspectives, and that's the kind of mindset we try to promote here and in our local communities."

"We believe that our position represents the vast majority of the church, even if it is not perceived that way in our particular dioceses," said Dr. Joan Gundersen of Progressive Episcopalians of Pittsburgh.

Organizers said all of the groups would consult with their own members in coming weeks about how to move forward as a group.

Fear Is Not the Word

Most of the groups are located in dioceses that have joined or are considering membership in the newly formed Network of Anglican Communion Dioceses and Parishes, which is seeking to provide "alternative episcopal oversight" for dissenting congregations in moderate-to-liberal dioceses. Via Media leaders said they think the Network's ultimate goal is to replace the Episcopal Church entirely within the Anglican Communion, and that, if not opposed, its actions may result in schism.

"Fear is not the word, but we pray that will not happen," said Gundersen.

Members of some of the groups reported that the level of anger and even "hatred" in their dioceses has increased in recent months. Some told of clergy and bishops refusing to be seen with those who did not agree with them on joining the Network, and of a rector who refused to wear vestments made by a woman who opposed his position. "It's Donatism in a modern form," said Dixie Hutchinson of The Gathering in Dallas, referring to a North African heresy of the 4th–7th centuries.

Others, such as the Central Florida group, said their bishop has worked for tolerance of all opinions while standing firm on remaining within the Episcopal Church. "Bishop Howe has had lots of pressure," said John Townsend. "He has pressure from churches that want to leave, but he has stood very firmly about property and he is not going to let it go away."

Another member, Donna Bott, said a moderate clergyman told her he didn't feel at all intimidated by Howe, but did feel pressured by other priests, particularly on the diocesan email list for clergy. In fact, several leaders cited the Internet as a two-edged sword: a wonderful organizing tool, but at the same time, a frequent source of misinformation and ill feeling.

Unity "Not at All Costs, but at All Risks"

At the group's closing Eucharist, Atlanta Bishop Neil Alexander quoted missionary bishop Charles Henry Brent, saying, "Unity is not a luxury, but a necessity. We must work for the unity of the church, 'not at all costs, but at all risks.' "

"My sense of the House of Bishops meeting is that the Episcopal Church is alive and well and vigorous and committed to the mission and gospel of our Lord Jesus Christ, and let us have no doubt about that," said Alexander. "However, it was interesting to listen to person after person talk about the fact that, in their judgment, the church is broken.

"Friends, I don't believe the church is broken.... Virtually all of those who want the church to be different absented themselves from the table, and I think that Bishop Brent would have said, no matter what, you've got to take the risk of what it means to be in unity and fellowship — not in agreement, but in reconciliation."

Two observers from the Episcopal Church's Executive Council attended the meeting, and Presiding Bishop Frank Griswold sent a letter of greeting to the group. "These are challenging days for our church, and yet they contain within themselves an invitation to be the many membered body of the risen Christ in a deeper and fuller way," Griswold wrote. "Rooted and grounded in common prayer, our divergent points of view find their place of meeting and reconciliation in word and sacrament and a life shared in the service of the Gospel. The diverse center is the overwhelming reality of our church and its voice is urgently needed, both within the church and in our fractured and polarized world."

Jan Nunley is deputy director of Episcopal News Service.

9

Jesus Cast Out the Demons, Not the People

Lillian Daniel

On my first day of a seminary internship, I walked the halls of the Mental Health Center with tentative steps. At this inpatient facility in a New England college town, university professors sat next to the homeless in the common area, bound only by their shared struggles with mental illness.

My steps and my fear carried me quickly to the safety of my supervisor's office, where I asked, "What am I supposed to be doing in this internship anyway? Frankly, I don't see what I can do to help these people before their medications kick in."

"Just wander the floor," she told me. "Talk to the patients. Make conversation."

I was horrified. Making conversation at church coffee hours is hard enough. The idea of making conversation in a mental hospital set my heart beating fast.

"Can't I lead a spirituality program or a worship service?" I asked.

"You'll do that eventually," she said. "But why don't you start by leaving this office and going out to talk to that gentleman?"

I looked out her office window to see a lone man rocking back and forth on a couch, muttering and shaking his head as if to disagree with his own last comment. The idea of making conversation with

---

Reprinted from *DisciplesWorld*.

someone who was already making conversation with himself did not appeal to me, but I ventured out.

It turns out he was quite willing to talk, but I soon found myself drowning in his flood of words about angels, an angry God, and the CIA. At first I tried correcting him; later, I would learn that my role was not to point out the difference between fact and fiction, but to listen. I learned to listen to conspiracy theories that made me laugh, to paranoid worries that made me sad, and to ideas about God that made me cringe.

How cruel it seemed that people in the grip of delusion often turned to God, only to dredge up some punishing vision. How interesting that the deluded seemed to relate to the devil so much more strongly than those we call sane. In my Protestant upbringing, I'd never once heard a sermon about Jesus casting out demons, but that was the story they wanted to talk about on the floor.

Because I was a chaplain, patients sometimes confided in me the things they couldn't tell the rest of the staff. "I'm only telling you this because you're a woman of God," the rocking man told me that first day. "Whatever you do, avoid the drinking fountains on this floor. The water is poisoned."

In staff team meetings, I learned as much about medical culture as I did about mental illness. While we called ourselves a "team," the hospital hierarchy made church hierarchy look like the work of amateurs. It was easy to see the tensions among the different healers, from the aides to the social workers to the nurses to the psychiatrist, who shared with many of the patients a habit of wearing dark sunglasses indoors.

At first I suspected chaplains were at the bottom of the hierarchy; some of the medical staff seemed ready to hand off the delusional patients to anyone who professed faith. After all, we both talked about and trusted in things unseen. But I soon realized that others on the staff took faith seriously and felt called to their healing work.

At one point, a labor dispute erupted and I heard about the ill effects of short staffing and hierarchy for its own sake, about how hard it is to work under such conditions. I learned that many in the field put up with the bureaucracy by God's grace and see their work as a ministry. I found myself walking in a union demonstration with workers and running into former patients, once again homeless on the streets. Both groups seemed confused that a chaplain would be there marching, but I was learning in that institutional setting that Christianity is an earthy religion, concerned with both the heartache and healing in everyday life.

After weeks of wandering the halls, making small talk amid the bizarre talk, I finally got to lead my first worship service. A small group gathered in a dark conference room, the usual lively mix you find in a mental health facility — professionals and parents, street people and suicide attempters, addicts and the alienated. One large woman had come to the room early and set up on the table an elaborate paper construction of postcards and clippings, every photograph featuring Princess Grace of Monaco.

I took a deep breath and began to read my carefully prepared sermon on Galatians. A man began to cough and then shake. A woman shifted in boredom. A cocaine addict interrupted me.

"Are we allowed to ask questions?" he said in the middle of my remarks. I nodded, keeping my finger on the page so as not to lose my place in the sermon.

"Exactly how long is this part going to last?" he asked.

Now the large woman felt free to interject. "I'd like for us to pray to Princess Grace," she said.

"Well, certainly, we can pray for the world's leaders, and we will pray for Princess Grace as well," I said.

"I don't want to pray *for* Princess Grace," she said, gesturing to her makeshift altar. "I said I wanted to pray *to* Princess Grace."

"Well, we're not going to," I explained gently. "We pray *for* Princess Grace. We pray *to* God."

"Well, give me one good reason for that," she said.

By now I had lost my place in the notes for good. With the theological narcissism of a seminarian, I wondered what God was telling me about my future in parish ministry in this, my first sermon ever.

I have since decided all preachers should be trained this way. On any given Sunday at church, the gospel word competes with the garbled words of interior voices that drown out God's love for so many in the pews. That day in the hospital, the voices were loud. The questions stretched me to new depths as I realized that pat answers and rules just wouldn't suffice.

Later as a pastor in that city, I sometimes bumped into former patients on the street, looking bedraggled and confused. I also bumped into former patients at their jobs or in restaurants or in my church, looking fresh and new. I carried this knowledge into the parish and remembered, when praying for healing, to include prayers for those with psychiatric issues alongside those for folks with cancer or heart conditions — illnesses our culture is more comfortable talking about. And I discovered a surprise in the Christian practice of visiting the sick: I am just as likely to be called to the psychiatric unit as the cardiac floor, but our culture's discomfort keeps one hospital stay a secret while another is made public. I pray for the day when that is not so. When the arms of the church can open wide enough to embrace those who pray *to* Princess Grace rather than *for* her, we follow in the footsteps of Jesus, who cast out the demons, but never the people.

Lillian Daniel is senior minister of the First Congregational Church (UCC) in Glen Ellyn, Illinois.

10

Pieta

Colombian Mother Cries for Activist Son Accused of Terrorism

Alexa Smith

LOUISVILLE — Eli Maria Alvarez can't stop crying.

Between sobs, bits of information blubber out. Yes, her son, Mauricio, had seemed more nervous, quieter, in the days before he was arrested. But she couldn't get him to talk. Yes, he slept less. No, he didn't go to the office as often.

The last time she saw him, she says, they were both in a cramped, Barranquilla jail cell, and he told her to agree to this interview. To let people know that *if* he is released, he will need a visa to get out of the country — and will need a place to go.

She adds this new concern to the why-is-he-late, what-has-gone-wrong, what-if-he's-hurt, what-if-he-doesn't-come home litanies that keep her awake at night.

She says she was always worried about him, afraid for him, her law-student son who worked for poor people for free. Her youngest of three. The baby. The poet. The idealist.

Now he's locked in a cell with three men who would cause any mother to lose sleep. The cell stinks. The food is lousy. He didn't have a bed, so she dragged a roll-away cot to the jail and set it up for him.

Reprinted from Presbyterian News Service.

Now he's telling her that he can never go back to public school. And he certainly can't go back to human-rights work.

"He needs to make a new start someplace else," she says.

This is almost too much. She has been afraid that he would disappear. Now he's telling her that, even if he is released, even if his lawyers show that there is no evidence to convict him of terrorism or subversion or any of the other awful things he is accused of, she will lose him anyway. Even if he gets out of jail, he will still be out of her reach.

It dizzies her to think that *this* is the best-case scenario.

Her translator, Presbyterian Church (USA) missionary Alice Winters, stops talking and says, "She's weeping."

In the background, Eli Maria's daughter, Renata, murmurs endearments softly in Spanish. A man clears his throat. Winters, who is translating in her third-floor apartment in a Barranquilla high-rise, says that, from now on, Mauricio's siblings, Renata, 25, and Moises, 29, will have to do the talking. It's too much for their mother.

The family crowds around a telephone on Winters' desk. The phone at home isn't safe. Eli Maria is sure that it is tapped.

This family has a huge problem. Mauricio Avilez Alvarez, 24, is charged with terrorism, subversion and murder. He's a law student who works on the campus of the Presbyterian Church of Colombia, helping some of Colombia's six million displaced families apply for government aid and document human-rights violations.

Barranquilla, like Colombia's other big cities, is ringed with camps full of refugees, but no one calls them that because they haven't crossed any borders. They're "displaced" — unable to go home — but still in Colombia. Most fled violence; and because the people behind the violence control the regions they left, they can't go back. So they sit. With little work, no money, few hopes.

Few cities welcome this kind of financial burden. And in Colombia, a paranoid logic argues that, if these people were forced off their land, they must be the dangerous ones. And if they're here, they must be guerrillas-in-disguise ready to infiltrate the cities, waiting for the right moment to unleash terror. But most are just people trying to get by.

And most of them are barely doing that.

Moises clears his throat.

Yes, the volunteer lawyers that Mauricio organized on behalf of Colombia's displaced are working frantically to get him out of jail. An appeal has even been sent to the attorney general's office in Bogota, but there has been no word. They have hired a new lawyer, but the case seems to have stalled somewhere in the system.

In Colombia, human-rights workers, union leaders, church leaders — anyone who can be tarred with a left-wing label — is in jeopardy of arrest. Mauricio is accused of being a guerrilla. He is accused of planting a bomb that exploded a few blocks from the synod office, injuring dozens of people.

Human-rights workers say his arrest is typical. It is a way to silence groups who are critical of new government policies intended to fight terrorism, but also smother civil liberties.

If the accused is released, he becomes an easy target for paramilitaries who often silence "subversives" with well-aimed shots.

There is no way that Mauricio has done what he's accused of, says Moises, who, to his mother's dismay, has taken over Mauricio's job as director of CEDERHNOS, a human-rights center where volunteer law students do field work with displaced persons.

"No, no, no, no, no, no," he says.

The day the bomb exploded, he says, Mauricio was in the office on the synod campus all day.

Right now, Moises is concerned about his brother's health and safety in jail.

He accepts that his brother, if he is released, must leave Colombia.

"Right from the beginning, everybody realized that leaving the country was an option, even his lawyers.... If he ever gets out of jail, every paramilitary group will have him in their sights, as someone to be dealt with."

Winters translates that phrase bluntly: "They'll try to kill him."

"The purpose of all this is to teach people that nobody should be a human-rights defender, nobody should get into this work in the first place," Moises says. "That's a problem. So, we've got to have a Plan A (to get Mauricio out of jail), and then a Plan B (to get him out of the country)."

The word on the street, Moises says, is that his accuser is a paid informant named Luis Enrique Meneses Pedraza, who testifies against others as part of a federal amnesty program.

Mauricio was picked up after a doctor's appointment in June. The doctor called his family. The family moved fast to protect him, lining up lawyers.

Moises says that, if he gets out of jail and leaves the country, Mauricio may be able to come back in two or three years. Maybe things will be cooled off by then.

He says that his brother would like to finish his legal studies. A Catholic, he'd like to study theology, too. In fact, he's spending his jail time reading the dozens of books his family brings to the prison: novels, poetry, theology. He's writing his own poetry, something he's always done.

The brothers, Moises and Maurico, have shared a room since they were little boys. They did until the day Mauricio was arrested. At work and at home, they looked out for each other, according to Moises. He's still trying to do that.

His mother says that she's praying to the Virgin Mary to help her boy.

She says she knew something was wrong long before anything actually happened. She knows now that Mauricio had heard rumors among displaced people that officials were asking questions about him and his work. He was depressed. But he didn't say much.

Renata says her brother always tried to protect his mother.

Renata says she doesn't feel safe herself, nowadays. She knows that police could search the house at any moment. Sometimes she thinks someone is following her in the street. But she isn't sure.

It is a disorienting mess, her mother agrees. "Everything that's happening, I get it all mixed up in my head," she says. "I knew this was risky. But it was a mission he had to do.... I understand that he wanted to work with the poor, to help people without help.

"He was always a good boy."

And then she starts crying again.

Alexa Smith is freelance writer living in Louisville, Kentucky.

11

Revival Turns Longstanding Rupture into Reconciliation

Andrea Higgins

CONOVER, N.C. (BP) — Sixteen years ago, Lanette Harris was caught in the middle.

She felt torn by the bitter division at Springs Road Baptist Church in Hickory, N.C., a town in the foothills of the Blue Ridge Mountains. Her roots ran deep at Springs Road, where her grandparents, parents and many other family members attended.

Her husband, Bill, however, felt the Lord leading them to join about 150 church members to break off from Springs Road and form their own church.

A rancorous disagreement had spiraled out of what some describe as a generational test of wills. What began as a difference of opinion between the new, well-liked, innovative pastor — who brought much growth and change to the church — and a beloved, longtime music director, spilled over into the membership.

New ideas clashed with tradition, said Bill Harris. No compromise could be found, and the pastor resigned in the fray.

Those who had taken his side founded New Life Baptist Church in neighboring Conover, eventually settling in a building just four miles from the old church in Hickory. The exiting pastor, however, did not join them.

Reprinted from *Baptist Press News*.

Revival Turns Longstanding Rupture into Reconciliation

Lanette Harris was among the charter members at New Life. "I was going under the authority of my husband where the Lord wanted us to be. It was a very, very difficult time when the split happened. I was emotionally wrought. It's something I hope I never have to go through again," she said, echoing the sentiments of many who remember those bitter days.

The Harrises long ago made amends with Lanette's family and other church members, who understood their decision. But, for all these years, the split left lingering resentment over the emotional and financial devastation caused by the departure of such a significant segment of the church membership. In the community, the perception was of a house divided.

Rather than let the longstanding resentment fester any longer, New Life members this year offered an olive branch to their former church home, inspired by a marathon revival that surprised the break-off congregation and softened hearts to heal old wounds.

Bill Harris, a deacon at New Life, was among those who thought it was time to put it right, although no one anticipated the change would come from a revival meeting.

New Life member Mary Larson admits she had no great expectations and was even a bit skeptical at the prospect of keeping people engaged for 10 straight days of revival.

She certainly didn't think she'd be asking for more, along with many others in the fellowship.

"We said, 'Oh, we don't want this to stop!'" Larson said, after being part of an invigorating 10 days that brought revival in the true sense of the word.

Seeing the profound outpouring, the Life Action revival team, visiting from Buchanan, Mich., stayed on to preach an extra day that was to have been a day of rest before traveling to their next engagement.

Still, the congregation wanted more.

New Life's pastor, Steve Clark, was so moved by the unexpected outpouring in the church that he kept the revival meetings going, preaching for 35 days, staring in March and ending in April.

The spiritual marathon took on a life of its own, as person after person shared how God was working.

"It just fell like a rock," Clark said. "There was such a spirit of brokenness and repentance. You could hear sobbing. It was about forgiveness. It just permeated the congregation. We met every night of the week. It was incredible. It wasn't an outpouring of spiritual awakening so much as it was revival — God's people returning to Christian life."

Larson said people were healed and family members who had been prayed for over the course of years came to Christ.

"People I never thought would share came up and would encourage you to share. God was doing some mighty things. We said, 'Whoa! God is here.' You just couldn't wait to get there every night. We would hang around after the meetings. We didn't want to leave each other. We just bonded," Larson said.

Though Clark has only been at the church for 11 years and, like most now at New Life, wasn't part of the rift that broke apart Springs Road, he was aware of the painful history. Occasionally through the years the pastor had brought up the idea of making amends, but people weren't ready. After the revival, however, when he broached the subject, most everyone enthusiastically agreed.

Clark asked for the few remaining charter members to discuss the possibility of issuing a formal, written apology to Springs Road Baptist Church for any harm or hurt caused by New Life's departure in 1988.

"The revival just broke everyone. They felt very sensitive to sin, any sin. That's where the seed was planted. I asked the Lord if there was anything we hadn't done, and the Lord spoke to me. 'There is one thing, Steve,'" Clark recounted.

Clark personally delivered the letter to his colleague and friend, Arthur Yount, who has been Springs Road's pastor for eight years. Yount shared the letter with the church, which had never recovered the membership it lost in the exodus and, for a time, had struggled to meet its financial obligations.

Not only did they accept the humble apology, they reciprocated. Members of Springs Road wanted to be forgiven for any hard feelings they contributed during the split as well.

"There's no such thing as a completely innocent party," Yount said. "God never orchestrates division."

In September, a full-page newspaper advertisement in *The Hickory Daily Record* announced an upcoming reconciliation service between the two churches. In the ad, they publicly requested and gave forgiveness. Their humility extended to the public, to which they offered contrition and made a joint apology for the poor Christian witness their breakup had been in the community.

"Repentance and forgiveness are the core of who we are," Yount said.

Instead of being known as churches that were at odds, they publicly sought reconciliation as one in Christ in the community, and the action to close a traumatic chapter in their church history has garnered many positive comments from non-church members.

Larson, who was among those intent on leaving in 1988, said she thought it was the right thing to do at the time but now knows it was wrong.

"We should have prayed through it and made it work," Larson said.

At the reconciliation service, Yount preached from Nehemiah about restoration. Members from each church joined together to sing in the choir. For members of both churches, a burden was lifted.

The two churches shared a Thanksgiving-eve service, and seniors from both churches have begun to share excursions, including luncheons and a Christmas celebration dinner at Springs Road, with more joint efforts to follow.

Larson said the revival that inspired the reconciliation has had a lasting effect in the daily worship of New Life members. Four prayer groups started meeting on various days in members' homes, and it is hoped they will lead to other groups.

For her daughter, it was great to walk down the halls of the old church where she had attended Sunday School as a child.

"It's just opened up doors. It's so wonderful. These people that were my friends, it's so wonderful to see them again," Larson said. "I found out that publicly going to someone and saying, 'Will you forgive me?' is a very freeing thing in your life. It's changed my life."

It has also changed her church.

"I did a discipleship program — going through and forgiving people and asking forgiveness for past wrongs, and that changed my life. It freed me up. I know it's the same principle for the church," Larson said.

"It's amazing when you get rid of it, how wonderful it feels," she said. "You can receive those blessings when all that junk is gone."

"I feel like God will really bless New Life for what they have done," said Annie Lee Lafone, 81, a charter member of Springs Road back in the 1950s.

Lafone stayed on during the exodus in 1988, which even saw the departure of her daughter. She remained friends with those who left, but saw hard feelings break up other friendships. Springs Road, which can seat 600 in the chapel, and was having tremendous growth before the split, now sees only about 160 at Sunday services.

"It's a sad story, but I think God's going to straighten it out," Lafone said.

Looking back on what the battle was about, Lafone calls the issue "nothing."

"A little old misunderstanding — the devil can take it and really make use of it," she said.

By the same token, looking at the formation of two churches after the traumatic events — New Life and Tri-City, a large church that has outpaced both of its predecessors, with a membership in the thousands — along with the recent reconciliation, Lafone said: "God can take bad things and make them turn into good."

Andrea Higgins is a freelance writer living in Raleigh, North Carolina.

12

When It Comes to Music, Christian Teens, Too, Are Pirates

Adelle M. Banks

The Gospel Music Association has embarked on a campaign to counter music piracy after commissioning a study that found purchasers of Christian music are as likely as other teens to engage in the practice.

Overall, the online survey of 1,449 teenagers found 80 percent of teenagers surveyed had engaged in at least one kind of music piracy — such as making copies of CDs for other people, downloading unauthorized free music or uploading music files to the Internet to share with others — in the past six months. Only 8 percent said unauthorized downloading and copying CDs for others was morally wrong.

But it was the more specific findings about Christian youth that association officials found disappointing, if not surprising.

Researchers found that 77 percent of born-again Christian teens engaged in music piracy compared to 81 percent of all other teens. Statistics for teen buyers of gospel, worship or contemporary Christian music were in the same range.

"On a gut level we had hoped that it would be true that Christian teens did have a little bit more of a moral stake in this issue,"

Reprinted from Religion News Service.

said Tricia Whitehead, spokeswoman for the Nashville, Tenn.–based music association, in an interview. "We hope that we can set ourselves apart a little bit and, in this case, we didn't."

With sales flat this year and down 5 percent last year, members of the Christian music industry suspected that they, along with the rest of the music world, were the victims of piracy, she said.

The association used the survey to help shape a new effort it kicked off on Sunday (April 25) at the start of its annual GMA Week, a time when members of the Christian music industry gather in Nashville for meetings and an awards ceremony.

"This furthers our resolve that we, meaning the industry, parents and spiritual leaders, need to do a better job educating the hearts and minds of young people to the basic biblical principle, 'thou shalt not steal,'" said GMA President John Styll at a news conference announcing the "Millions of Wrongs Don't Make It Right" campaign.

The association has developed a five-page brochure — something they do want to be downloaded — that can be posted on artists' Web sites and available at their concerts.

"Most of us would never even consider stealing something — say, a picture or a piece of clothing — from a friend's house," the brochure reads. "Yet when it comes to stealing digital recordings of copyrighted music, people somehow seem to think the same rules don't apply.... Contrary to popular opinion, illegally downloading or copying copyrighted music is the same as stealing; there is no difference."

The brochure goes on to list criminal penalties — as high as $250,000 in fines or five years in prison — and recommends uninstalling peer-to-peer software mostly used for illegal downloading, such as KaZaA, and opting for authorized Web sites instead.

It also features quotations and photographs of artists Steven Curtis Chapman, Stacie Orrico and Shaun Groves, who give their perspective on the matter.

"Students I've spoken with adopt a Robin Hood complex, saying they're stealing from wealthy people and therefore it's not wrong," Groves said. "The reality is that my wife and two kids live in an apartment. We drive 10-year-old Camrys, not BMWs."

Chapman and Orrico said that the money paid for CDs doesn't just help the artists and record companies but everyone down the line in the CD-making process, from engineers to the truck drivers who transport the music to the stores.

While Christian music industry officials reacted especially to the survey's findings about Christian teens who are involved in piracy, a key researcher on the project was concerned about the overall findings.

"I was surprised that there was not a higher proportion of teenagers that believed music piracy was wrong," said David Kinnaman, vice president of the Barna Group in Ventura, Calif.

"Particularly with all the focus that's been given to it based on the legal side of the argument."

His company designed the survey and analyzed the results. Harris Interactive, a market research firm based in Rochester, N.Y., collected the data for the survey in February that had an overall margin of error of plus or minus 3 percentage points.

Researchers found that teens were rarely getting moral advice about music downloading or CD copying from parents or church leaders.

"They've been influenced most often by their peers when it comes to just talking about this issue," Kinnaman said in an interview.

Whitehead said the Christian Music Trade Association, an affiliate of GMA that represents record companies, hopes to establish partnerships with retailers and radio stations to communicate to teens and their parents about the issue.

She emphasized that industry representatives aren't shunning technology but are asking teens to use legal services to download their preferred music.

"If they still want to continue on that idea that they can get one song and put together their own album, they can do that legally and at a higher quality and for a really reasonable cost," she said. "Most of the services are about 99 cents a song. You can make a full CD for 10 bucks."

Adelle M. Banks is Senior Correspondent for Religion News Service.

13

Politics and Polarization
Walt Wiltschek

Back in 1968, the United States was torn over a war halfway around the world, and public opinion was sharply divided. Richard Nixon was running for president that year and faced the dilemma of forging a constituency out of the nation's many diverse groups.

A 1971 speech journal article by Andrew King and Floyd Douglas Anderson examined the process of creating this "silent majority," accomplished through what they called "the rhetoric of polarization." They say it took another year after Nixon was elected to build his power base built by uniting people around a common enemy, in this case the opponents of the Vietnam War.

The result: A fragmented nation became highly polarized. The authors defined this act of polarization as "a process by which an extremely diversified public is coalesced into two or more highly contrasting, mutually exclusive groups sharing a high degree of internal solidarity" in some key belief(s).

The tactics to bring about this aim, they said, included building an "us-versus-them" mentality, belittling those who disagreed with Nixon's positions, and creating stereotypes and distrust. Vice president Spiro T. Agnew became the lead attack dog, calling foes of the administration "nattering nabobs of negativism," "pusillanimous pussyfooters," and other such colorful putdowns.

A whirlwind of charges and countercharges ensued, adding to what the authors called "a Babel of strident voices."

Reprinted from *Messenger*.

Sound familiar? Political pundits and analysts said the 2000 presidential election atmosphere was one of the most polarized the nation had seen in years. The 2004 election has had a similar feel, and the rhetoric from both sides has been strident, to put it mildly, once again. Charges and countercharges, playing on fears, attack ads, put-downs — it's not much of a model to follow, no matter which side one supports.

Unfortunately, the church seems to be following this model all too well. News reports have included all manner of biting quotes from church leaders who disagree with some person or group.

The Church of the Brethren has been playing the game pretty well, too. A variety of list servers, online journals, newsletters, and speeches seem to exhibit a growing tendency to attack and belittle rather than seeking to discern prayerfully in community. One or two issues may be driving the current war of words, but it's eventually about attitude and relationship.

We risk becoming a polarized church, if we're not there already. King and Anderson say an aim of polarization is to "move persons out of the ranks of the uncommitted and force them to make a conscious choice between one of the two competing groups." If a sense of unity around Jesus Christ cannot bring the ends closer together, the church's wide middle spectrum will be stretched painfully.

In a single day at the *Messenger* offices recently, we received a letter from a conservative Brethren demanding that we not print anything representing liberal viewpoints, while a progressive caller was upset that we published a letter representing a conservative perspective.

Both were told the same thing: *Messenger* is a meeting place for the church, where all its voices should be heard and weighed. Former Supreme Court Justice Oliver Wendell Holmes, in describing the United States as a "marketplace of ideas," observed "that it is hazardous to discourage thought, hope, and imagination; that fear breeds repression; that repression breeds hate."

One might hope the church at-large can hear one another out as fellow Christians, testing things with patience in the light of scripture so that we don't breed hate. It's OK to disagree, but not to shout. Prayer, not politics, should drive the church.

Another former president, Abraham Lincoln, once said, "A house divided against itself cannot stand." Is our house, like that of the foolish man in Jesus' parable, at risk of collapsing on the sand? Or will we build wisely? Let's pray it's the latter, and leave the "nattering nabobs" to others.

Walt Wiltschek is the editor of *Messenger*.

14

Hearts and Minds
The Power of Reconciliation
Jim Wallis

There is probably no more divisive time in America than an election season. So I thought it appropriate to tell a personal story of reconciliation that is very important to me, and one that I have never told before. It is about my relationship with a fellow Christian who, if he were still alive, would likely be voting differently than me in the upcoming election.

Bill Bright was the founder and president of Campus Crusade for Christ, an evangelical organization on campuses around the country. Motivated, above all else, by the Great Commission, Bill Bright wanted to reach every person on the planet for Christ "in this generation." Concerned about the "moral degeneration" of America, Bright wanted America to come back to God — which for him meant an ultra-conservative political agenda. Bill and I were both evangelical Christians, but we clearly disagreed on a whole range of political issues.

In 1976, Bill Bright joined a far-right member of Congress named John Conlan and other conservatives in a project to mobilize evangelical prayer and cell groups for political purposes. It was, in fact, the first attempt to create a "Religious Right" in American politics — several years before the founding of groups like the Moral Majority and the Christian Coalition.

Reprinted from *Sojourners*.

We at *Sojourners* decided to investigate. It became the most extensive investigative project we had ever undertaken, and resulted in a cover story in the magazine titled "The Plan to Save America." Bright was publicly embarrassed by our exposé and the whole experience. Though we had been scrupulously careful, backing up every fact in the story with at least three sources, Bright angrily denounced me. We invited Bright and the others involved to respond, both before and after the article was published, but they chose not to. Because we also differed on almost every political question from Vietnam to domestic issues, a bitter and public polarization grew up between Bill Bright and myself.

The bad blood continued for many years. I remember a particularly painful moment one year at a dinner for evangelical leaders, when Bright again went on the attack against me in a very public way, calling me a "liar."

More than two decades later, Bright and I found ourselves at yet another religious leaders' dinner. When I saw him across the room, I swallowed hard and headed in his direction. He obviously didn't recognize me after so long. I introduced myself, and he became quiet. I said, "Bill, I need to apologize to you. I was in a hotel several months ago and knew you were there too. I should have come to your room and tried to mend the painful breach between us after all these years. I didn't do that, and I should have. I'm sorry."

The now-old man reached out and wrapped his arms around me. Then he said, "Jim, we need to come together. It's been so long, and the Lord would have us come together." We both had tears in our eyes and embraced for a long time. Then Bill said, "Jim, I'm so worried about the poor, about what's going to happen to them. You're bringing us together on that, and I want to support you." I was amazed. We agreed to get together soon.

A few months later, Bill and I were again, coincidentally, at the same hotel. I called Bill and we agreed to a walk on the beach together the next morning. Bill and I shared our own conversion stories. We shared our callings and dreams for our respective ministries, and how we might be more connected. Bill then astounded me, saying, "You know, Jim, I'm kind of a Great Commission guy." I smiled and nodded my head. "And I've discovered that caring for the poor is part of the Great Commission, because Jesus instructed us to 'teach the nations to observe all the things I have commanded you.' And Jim, Jesus certainly taught us to care for the poor, didn't he? Caring for the poor is part of the Great Commission!" said Bill Bright. When we got back to the hotel, Bill asked if we could pray together. We sat down and grasped each other's hands. First praying for each other, we also prayed for each other's ministries. Bill Bright prayed for me, and for the work of Call to Renewal and *Sojourners*. When we were finished, he said he wanted to raise some money for our "work of the Lord."

Bill, who was now more than 80 years old, soon began to get sick. I kept track of how he was doing. Then one day, I got a letter — from Bill Bright. Here's what the letter said:

> My Dear Jim,
> Congratulations on your great ministry for our Lord. I rejoice with you. An unexpected gift designated to my personal use makes possible this modest contribution to your magazine. I wish I had the means to add at least three more zeros to the enclosed check. Warm affection in Christ. Yours for helping to fulfill the Great Commission each year until our Lord returns. Bill

Inside the letter was a check for $1,000.

As I was reading Bill's letter, my colleague Duane Shank walked into my office. "Did you hear?" he asked. "Bill Bright just died." We looked at the postmark on the letter and compared it to the news reports of Bill's death. We concluded that writing me this letter was one of the last things that Bill Bright did on earth. Bill sent a $1,000 gift to the magazine that had exposed his most embarrassing moment more than 30 years before, as an affirmation of the ministry of another Christian leader who he once regarded as his enemy. I couldn't hold back the tears, and can't again as I write down this story for the first time.

The experience of my relationship with Bill Bright has taught me much about the promise and power of reconciliation. I will never again deny the prospect of coming together with those with whom I disagree. It is indeed the power of the gospel of Jesus Christ to break down the walls between us. Thank you, Bill. I will never forget you.

Jim Wallis is editor-in-chief of *Sojourners*.

15

Deciphering the Passion

A Guide to What's Biblical and What's Not in Mel Gibson's Movie

Scot McKnight

Christians have never felt obligated to support, let alone defend, a Hollywood production of biblical events. Nor have the faithful felt any need to stand by the directors and actors in such movies as sharing their faith. But Cecil B. DeMille is not Mel Gibson, and Moses is not Jesus. And *The Ten Commandments* is not *The Passion of the Christ*.

The stakes are higher, the rhetoric more intense, and evaluation of the movie less objective. The subject is the execution of Yeshua — and it struck me as odd that people could munch on popcorn and drink pop as they watched an event that changed history.

The Passion of the Christ, with its air of super-realism, is unforgettable: its images sear into the mind, leaving its viewers in stunned silence and wondering an assortment of "whys?" I predict the movie will become a classic and will shape the minds of a generation. Because it will shape minds, we need to be especially aware of what we are viewing.

Christians, it needs to be emphasized, defend the Gospels and not cinematic representations of those Gospels. Leaders in the church have said this movie affords an incomparable opportunity for evangelism and for instruction. True. What is also true is that the church

---

Reprinted from *The Covenant Companion.*

also has an unparalleled opportunity to clarify the role the passion narratives played in the most sordid catastrophe of modern history — the Holocaust. We can do the former without neglecting the latter.

Gibson and the Bible

It might be useful to remind ourselves what we are viewing in *The Passion of the Christ*.

First, there is plenty that is biblical. Jesus appears in the eerie late night light in Gethsemane crying out to Abba (Father) in Aramaic. Judas betrays Jesus and hangs himself. Jesus is thrust before the authorities; he is moved from authority to authority; Peter denies Jesus; the other disciples remain at a distance from Jesus; Pilate comes off as arrogant, while his wife is worrisome; among the Jewish priests there is confusion, chaos, and accusation; we meet Simon of Cyrene; Jesus carries the cross part of the way and then needs help; Jesus is crucified; Jesus is raised. All this (and more) is biblical.

Second, there are a number of elements of the movie that are not biblical. Some of what is not in the Bible perhaps happened; some of it probably or certainly did *not* happen. Some of it is innocent and some of it maybe not. Some of it derives from medieval legends. The following did not come from the Bible.

> On the march from Gethsemane to the authorities Jesus is beaten (perhaps) and tossed over a bridge and suspended by his chains (legendary).
>
> Mary is called "Mother" by the disciples before the cross (probably not).
>
> Mary Magdalene is identified with the woman caught in sin in John 8 (certainly not).
>
> Mary, Mary Magdalene, and John watch everything up close throughout the entire movie (certainly not).

The Roman soldiers are vicious and brutal (probably) and demented (probably not).

The Jewish priestly leadership comes off as crazed with some having what looks like blood on their teeth (too much for me).

Jesus is beaten bloody beyond belief (we don't know how severe the beatings were but his need of Simon and his premature death suggest it was severe).

Pilate's wife comes off as a follower of Jesus (legendary) and gives to Mary a white cloth to wipe up the blood of Jesus (legendary).

Jesus speaks to Pilate in Latin (very doubtful).

Jesus falls a few times on the Via Dolorosa (perhaps) under a monstrous cross (legendary, he probably carried the cross beam only).

A woman (the legendary Veronica) gives Jesus a cloth to wipe his face (certainly not).

Mary, Mary Magdalene, and John attend Jesus after his death (certainly not, this was done by Nicodemus and Joseph of Arimathea).

Third, Gibson introduces some interpretive devices. In any movie gaps have to be jumped and interpretation comes in to give the accounts continuity and color. What Gibson adds is credible, even if I may demur here and there.

Satan weaves in and out of scenes. Flashbacks in the movie (Jesus as a carpenter making a table with legs; Jesus falling as a boy and Mary running to him) set up the emotion of contexts. When Jesus dies the winds pick up and the clouds swirl. The Father sheds a tear of love for his son (and world). In the (all too) brief resurrection scene, the sun appears and the healed Son takes one step.

Fourth, there are some problems that confuse history, faith, and tradition. I mention four. Gibson has the body of Jesus beaten to a pulp. Most would agree that Gibson operates out of a specific pre–Vatican II Roman Catholic tradition. In that tradition physical suffering atones and the depth of human sin requires massive physical suffering. This sort of *quid pro quo* skews what the atonement is all about.

Satan's presence in *The Passion of the Christ* is profound. When Jesus crushes the serpent's head in Gethsemane we are treated to a piece of imaginative theology that finds no rival in movie-making. But from then on Satan moves too often among the Jewish crowds and not enough among the Roman soldiers, Roman authorities, or Pilate and his wife. This is a mistake. Even more, I am persuaded that Satan ought to be "de-sexualized," but instead Satan is portrayed by a woman.

Jesus is removed from the cross by Mary, Mary Magdalene, and John. This, too, is a mistake. The Gospels state that the body of Jesus was removed by two Jewish council members who were in sympathy with Jesus: Nicodemus and Joseph of Arimathea. One of them appears in the scene, and plays a minor role.

One might say that the followers of Jesus, while they finally came forward at the cross and got close enough to hear Jesus, had been keeping themselves at a distance to protect themselves. I doubt seriously that they got close enough to remove him from the cross.

No one walks away from this movie without thinking of gore and brutality. The paradox of Christianity is that God used this sort of death — probably less gruesome than Gibson depicts but nonetheless gruesome — to atone for human sin. Jesus acts compassionately on the Via Dolorosa as hints of God's love. Gibson creatively interprets the scene at Golgotha by flashbacks to the Last Supper, by appealing to John 14:6, and by doing what he can at the graphic level to show the scene as an act of grace. It is hard to make a crucifixion look like an act of grace. I give Gibson credit for trying. I'd like more on the resurrection.

Gibson's presentation cannot be mentioned without stating that he used details from the nineteenth-century stigmatic and mystic Anne

Catherine Emmerich, as recorded in her book *The Dolorous Passion of Our Lord Jesus Christ*. She recorded her own visions of the last week, which were often akin to medieval legends, and Gibson thinks her visions valuable enough to use in his movie.

Three examples: Emmerich depicts the Garden scene as a contest between Jesus and Satan; she relates Jesus' hanging over the bridge; and she speaks of Pilate's wife giving Mary white cloths. Call it creative license. What you can't make of it is faithfulness to the Gospels.

Gibson and the Jews

Is *The Passion of the Christ* anti-Semitic? To charge Gibson with anti-Semitism means he despises Jews because of their race. He has denied this and no one has come up with an instance to show he is anti-Semitic.

To charge the movie with being anti-Semitic is to accuse the movie of castigating Jews because of their race. I'm also confident this is not true. He picks on the priestly leaders, not the people.

To claim the movie will be used for anti-Semitic purposes means that some will use the movie against Jews because of their race. Of this, I am certain. There are senseless, bigoted people in our world, some of whom hate Jews for no reasons other than that they are Jews. They will find in this movie grist for their evil grindings.

Could Gibson have been more balanced and more sensitive? Of this I am certain. We live in a post-Holocaust age, in an age that is coming away from centuries of passion plays in Europe that incited violent anti-Semitism. As Christians we have an obligation — because we believe God loves all people, because we are to love all people — to present the Gospels as sensitively as we can while remaining true to the biblical record.

I would have asked Gibson not to include Matthew 27:25 ("let his blood be on us") — it was in a preview I saw and it remains in the movie in Aramaic without subtitles. This text can only be used with careful commentary and clear explanations of what it meant and what it no longer means. It would take a long scene to clarify this text. I would also have made a big deal out of Joseph of Arimathea and Nicodemus at the cross to show that there were Jewish leaders who disagreed with those who judged Jesus seditious.

The theology of this movie concerns me at times: the atonement is too physical for me; there is too much Mary (and I love her more than most Protestants); Veronica is a legend; the trip to the cross looks like the Stations of the Cross.

Why are so many Christians defensive? Why the insistence, some by my academic friends, that this movie is historically accurate down to the details? Why? Because Mel Gibson has the courage to spend his own money for an unabashedly Christian movie. We live in an age when the public square is not congenial to the Christian gospel, and when anyone bucks Hollywood conservatives are ready to stand in line for a piece of the action — even if it requires accepting legends and interpretations that many find unusual.

But, let us agree on this: it is time to stop talking about the man who made the movie and talk about the Man who is the movie.

Scot McKnight is professor of biblical and theological studies at North Park University in Chicago. He is the author of *The Jesus Creed: Loving God, Loving Others* (Paraclete, 2004).

16

Adventist Church Joins Coalition against Worldwide Human Trafficking

Sandra Blackmer

To help raise awareness among church members worldwide of the horror and prevalence of human trafficking, the Seventh-day Adventist Church has joined a coalition of nonprofit organizations, under the director of the U.S. Department of Health and Human Services, that are committed to eradicating this international inhumanity.

Ralph Benko and Kari Rai, consultants to the U.S. Department of Health and Human Services (HHS), met at the church's world headquarters in Silver Springs, Maryland, on November 3, 2004, with General Conference (GC) Women's Ministries director and associate director Ardis Stenbakken and Heather-Dawn Small, GC Public Affairs and Religious Liberty (PARL) assistant director James Standish, GC Children's Ministries director Linda Koh, and PARL specialist Viola Hughes. The GC representatives agreed to share information with those in their departments and, consequently, the entire Adventist Church membership, about human trafficking and how to find help for victims of this practice.

"We've been working with human trafficking issues for maybe 10 years," said Stenbakken, who explained that she first became aware of the dimensions of the problem when she attended the 1995 United Nations Fourth World Conference on Women in Beijing, China.

Reprinted from the *Adventist Review*.

"Between 800,000 and 900,000 people fall victim to human trafficking each year," said Benko. "About 18,000 to 20,000 are brought into the United States from Asia, Central and South America, and Eastern Europe. Victims of human trafficking are subjected to force, fraud, or coercion, for the purpose of sexual exploitation or forced labor."

"We are not talking about [just a] Third World problem," said Small. "It's everybody's problem."

According to government reports, many victims of human trafficking are forced to work in prostitution or the sex entertainment industry. But trafficking also involves labor exploitation, such as domestic, restaurant, janitorial, sweatshop factory, and migrant agricultural work. Some traffickers keep victims locked up; other traffickers instill fear in victims using methods such as debt bondage, threats of violence, confiscation of passports or other identification documents, isolation from family and friends, and telling victims they will be imprisoned or deported for immigration violations if they contact authorities. Trafficking of humans is estimated to be the second-largest criminal industry in the world after drug dealing, and the fastest growing. The U.S. State Department estimates human trafficking to be a $13 billion-per-year global industry.

As a result of inhumane living conditions, victims of trafficking often suffer from many physical and psychological health problems, such as HIV/AIDS; chronic back, hearing, cardiovascular, and respiratory problems from working in dangerous agriculture, sweatshop, or construction conditions; malnourishment; serious dental problems; tuberculosis; and psychological trauma. Often it is the children who suffer the most.

The Trafficking Victims Protection Act (TVPA) of 2000 was enacted to provide victims with a temporary visa, called a T-visa, which allows those freed from trafficking to remain in the U.S. for up to three years, with the opportunity to apply for residency. Prior to the enactment of TVPA, no comprehensive Federal law existed to protect victims of trafficking or to prosecute the traffickers, and many victims were being deported as illegal aliens. The U.S. Department of Health and Human Services (HHS) is designated as the agency responsible for helping victims of human trafficking become eligible to receive benefits and services, including food, health care, and employment assistance.

The problem, however, is that most trafficking victims don't know the law, and they need advocates to help them. That is why HHS has organized a new program, called the Rescue and Restore Victims of Trafficking Campaign, to heighten awareness of this abuse and to help people identify victims and give them information about where to get help. HHS is particularly targeting those who are more likely to come in contact with trafficking victims, such as vice officers, pastors, nonprofit workers, farmers, and emergency room attendants.

"Victims of trafficking require fast, safe, and reliable help," said Wade F. Horn, assistant secretary for Children and Families at HHS. "The Rescue and Restore Victims of Trafficking Campaign will educate the public on how they can assist, while giving victims the immediate aid they need."

In 2003, U.S. president George Bush signed legislation that authorized more than $200 million to be used by the federal government to combat the practice of human trafficking. At the United Nations General Assembly in September 2003, Bush said, "Nearly two centuries after the abolition of the transatlantic slave trade, and more than a century after slavery was officially ended, the trade in human beings for any purpose must not be allowed to thrive in our time."

U.S. Secretary of Health and Human Services Tommy G. Thompson, in a written statement in December 2003, said, "By signing the reauthorization of the federal human trafficking program, the president is reaffirming his administration's commitment to end the horror of human trafficking, and to ensure that the real criminals — the traffickers of innocent people — are persecuted to the fullest extent of the law."

"Human trafficking is one of the most pressing human rights challenges of our time," said the Honorable Denise L. Majette, U.S.

Representative for the Fourth Congressional District of Georgia, during the inauguration of the Rescue and Restore program in Atlanta in April 2004. "It will take vigilant citizenry to fight the criminals who turn the lives of so many into living nightmares."

According to HHS Trafficking in Persons program director Steve Wagner, a Trafficking Information and Referral Hotline connects social service providers, law enforcement, and potential trafficking victims to local organizations that determine whether someone is a victim and provide services and benefits for victims. Operators who speak 150 languages are available to assist callers 24 hours a day, seven days a week.

"Rescue and Restore is very respectful of the international leadership that the Adventist Church has provided under the direction of Ardis Stenbakken long before it became a more widely known issue," said Benko. "The Adventists have been in the forefront [of dealing with this issue]."

"Early Adventists stood up against slave traders," said PARL assistant director James Standish. "Adventists today are once again standing up against those who make a trade of human beings. I am proud to be part of a church that doesn't simply sit on the sidelines wringing its hands when God's children are being brutally mistreated."

With more than 13 million members worldwide, and with an ethnically diverse membership "on the frontline," Benko says the Adventist Church can reach a wide variety of people with this message, and many members are working in positions in which there is a high likelihood of discovering human trafficking.

For more information about human trafficking, go to *www.acf.hhs.gov/trafficking*. To connect victims with someone in the United States who can help, call 1-888-373-7888.

Sandra Blackmer is the news editor of the *Adventist Review*

17

A Conservative Case for Gay Marriage

Rev. Matt Fitzgerald

Almost all of those in favor of gay marriage use the rhetoric of civil rights to champion their cause. While I wholeheartedly agree that legal, state-sanctioned marriage is a right that should be made available to same-sex couples I feel that case is already being made, and being made well. Instead, I want to suggest that if we do not embrace and practice gay marriage the Church will, in fact, encourage sexual sin.

This claim will not make sense if you reject the following bedrock assumption: homosexuality is an essential, ingrained dimension of a gay person's makeup. This, of course, is an explicit rejection of the Christian right's attempt to explain the origin of homosexuality.

In the Bible's most infamous comment on same-sex activity, Paul presumes that those who engage in gay sex engage in isolated acts of deviation from a universally shared heterosexual norm. "Men, giving up natural intercourse with women, were consumed with passion for one another" (Romans 1:27). In this understanding, homosexual activity is a choice heterosexuals make. Like a truth-teller deviating from honesty to tell a lie, a person engaged in gay sex momentarily departs from the morally preferable standard.

This was Paul's first-century Jewish worldview, and it is one adopted by contemporary Christians who label homosexuality a "lifestyle" and try to convert gays and lesbians into heterosexuality. Their efforts often fail spectacularly, as was the case when the two men who founded Exodus International, the most prominent of

Reprinted from *Christian Networks Journal*.

many "ex-gay" ministries, left the organization and divorced their wives to celebrate a gay marriage with one another.

Biblical literalists will, of course, label such sadly predictable events sinful and continue insisting that Paul's worldview still holds. To my mind, subscribing to a first-century sexual anthropology that modern understandings of human sexuality have refuted makes as much sense as believing the earth is flat because, as evidenced in Daniel 4:10, the ancient Hebrew cosmology assumed it so.

However, a belief in the essential nature of homosexuality is not primarily a negative response to the Christian right. Instead, first and foremost, it is a positive theological conviction. God creates some people gay, and because God declares creation good, homosexual people must therefore be good. This is not to say that the way homosexuality is practiced in our culture is uniformly moral. Indeed, as I'll go on to suggest, it can be quite immoral. But as Daniel Helminiak wisely notes, "like heterosexual acts, homosexual acts are neither right nor wrong in themselves. They can be used for good or evil, but in themselves they are neither."[1]

•

As a pastor I have married heterosexual couples who approach the altar with serious joy, moved and even unnerved by the role that God is playing in their bold promise of lifelong faithfulness. I have also married straight couples who see the Church as a cute marriage chapel, couples whose religiosity is frivolous at best, grooms who show up half-drunk to their own weddings, and brides who show more devotion to the perfect dress than the one true God. I have no data to verify this assumption, but my guess is that couples who appreciate the fact that God judges and supports their wedding vows stand a better chance at a successful union than those who ignore the divine dimension of marriage. But even newly-weds who mine deeper meaning from the schmaltzy pop song they choose for their wedding

---

1. Daniel A. Helminiak, *What the Bible Really Says about Homosexuality* (San Francisco: Alamo Square Press, 1994), 77.

reception's "first dance" than the Christian language in their wedding service, receive the church's blessing. For, although the Church's power over culture fades more every day, marriage in a sanctuary still validates and sanctions a couple's decision to be together. And even if a married couple trivializes God, this sanction stabilizes their relationship. This is why countless un-churched heterosexual couples come knocking at the Church's door each spring. Despite its abysmal failure rate, even in an age that idolizes celebrities who practice serial divorce, couples are more likely to be faithful within the institution of marriage than outside it.

•

C. S. Lewis wrote that the male sexual appetite "is in ludicrous and preposterous excess of its function."[2] The cause of this condition seems to have roots in the biological impulse to produce children, but it is inflamed by other factors. Our culture teaches that profound meaning can be found in pleasure. Sex can be among the most pleasurable of activities. Therefore, many American men grow up thinking that sex is the most important thing in the world. When combined with the objectification and commoditization of female bodies, the result can be devastating for women. But relations between the sexes are not the only ones scarred by our twisted appreciation of sex. Despite the fact that their sexual relations don't result in offspring, gay men are certainly not immune from our culture's insistence that the more sex a man has, the happier he will be.

Years ago I used to walk my dog on a beach that ran along the Mississippi River. The place was a hidden pocket of beauty inside a busy city. My typical practice was to walk at lunch-time, but one evening, I took the dog out near twilight. This beach was never crowded, but as night began to fall I crossed paths with several dozen men, walking alone. In my naivete I thought, "How strange, none of these guys are walking their dogs." Later I learned that the beach was among the

---

2. C. S. Lewis, *Mere Christianity* (New York: Macmillan, 1952), 96.

city's most popular venues for gay men desiring anonymous sex. It is easy to shake an indignant finger at such behavior, but as Christians we must remember that gay people are God's good creatures whose relationships we refuse to bless. When a person's sexuality is deemed deviant and he has to hide it, it is going to surface in an immoral fashion. By refusing to marry gay men and lesbian women the Church all but forces them to live in sin.

In our "if it feels good, do it" culture an argument against uncommitted sex may seem quaint, but it is very serious. In our role as the body of Christ the church is called to lift people up out of sin. By denying gays and lesbians the right to marry, Christianity encourages what Stanley Hauerwas and William H. Willimon call "the self-deceit and violence that seem inherent to sex without promise."[3] Those in the Church can pretend that beaches like the one I stumbled across don't exist, but, such destructive behavior will continue so long as we help perpetuate it.

Of course, countless same-sex couples are already in committed relationships. But more often than not, such faithfulness occurs despite the Church, not because of it. In June, following the Massachusetts Supreme Court decision legalizing same-sex marriage, the satirical newspaper *The Onion* published an article under the headline, "Gay Couple Feels Pressured to Marry." The fictional article reported a lesbian in a tenuous relationship saying, "It seems like just yesterday I was annoyed because straight people were awkwardly asking if we were 'friends' or 'partners.' Now, every convenience store clerk who guesses we're gay asks us if we're going to get married under the new law." Rather than working against such pressure, we could work with it. Today, the Church condemns millions of gay men and lesbian women to sex outside of marriage. Rather than helping cause such rampant sinfulness, we should lead the struggle against it. If we begin marrying our lesbian sisters and gay brothers, we will help them

---

3. Stanley Hauerwas and William H. Willimon, *The Truth About God: The Ten Commandments in Christian Life* (Nashville: Abingdon Press, 1999).

discover the chastening beauty of committed love. To do otherwise is to harm God's gay and lesbian children.

The Church should not underestimate its power in this situation. President Bush recently said, "the sacred institution of marriage should not be redefined by a few activist judges." What he forgets is that it is not our civil laws that make marriage sacred. The sacredness of love between two people is created by God, and announced by the Church. For this reason, despite their best intentions, "a few activist judges" will never be able to re-define the sanctity of marriage. On the other hand, hundreds of thousands of activist churches could work miracles.

Matt Fitzgerald is the pastor of Epiphany Church in Chicago and is the Senior Contributing Editor of *Christian Networks Journal*.

18

Treasures without Turmoil
Readers Advise How to Distribute Heirlooms after a Family Death

Julie B. Sevig

Granted, not every sibling has the same treasure tale as Mary Ann Johnson and her brother.

The Johnsons came from distant cities to clean out their parental home in Lubbock, Texas, after their mother's death. Their thoughtful, methodical way of working through the house in one week's time proved to be a success story.

"We chose easy tasks first, beginning with the linen closets," says Mary Ann Johnson, a member of Holy Trinity Lutheran Church, Lancaster, Pa. "We worked on, moving gradually to more difficult decisions. As tears sometimes flowed and possible conflicts entered the dynamic, we vowed that we wouldn't allow pain and hurt feelings to jeopardize our love and support of one another during this painful task."

They placed the most sentimental objects on a table in the family room. When all else was sorted, they returned to those items. "I chose, then he, until everything was gone," she says. "To this day we have some of these special items in our homes, and our relationship continued with new respect and affirmation for who each of us was in our adult life, having shared this common start."

Reprinted from *The Lutheran*.

Johnson and other survivors — of loved ones and of potential conflicts — responded to *The Lutheran*'s reader call for inventive ways to distribute goods after a family death.

A three-page e-mail with the subject line "family in pain" reminds us of the many testimonials of distribution gone wrong. But readers who answered this call had practical, even clever, advice for others. And, like Johnson, were proud of the way they or their loved ones had conducted themselves.

Think Ahead to Avoid Fussing

Peaceful distribution is often the result of foresight. So start now — put a name on it or make a list, readers say.

Harold Skillrud, a retired ELCA bishop in Atlanta, learned that advice years ago when visiting the congregational matriarch upon his arrival as pastor of Lutheran Church of the Redeemer, Atlanta.

He recalls: "Shortly after the visit began she made a strange request. 'Turn over that chair,' she commanded. I obeyed without question. 'What do you see?' 'A scrap of paper with a man's name,' I replied. 'That's my son. Now turn over that lamp.' Once more a scrap of paper was attached, this time with her daughter's name on it. 'Everything I own has a person's name attached. I know I won't be around long, and when I'm gone I don't want any family fussing.' "

"You First"

Well-aware of how many families end up in "heated battles and angry aftermaths," Lester and Nancy Polenz, Mount Gilead, Ohio, decided their way of keeping peace was to ask for nothing.

Ione Murdock already gives items to her two sons, including family stories with the treasures. "We admit such a stance meant that we missed out on some valuable and desirable things," wrote Lester, a retired pastor whose church membership remains at Shepherd of the Hills Lutheran, Sylva, N.C. "But as time passed, we realized that nothing was worth any conflict or confusion that might have resulted from our insisting on our rights to what we wanted or treasured.

"To not insist on our rights or wishes went against the grain, yet we have never regretted taking that stance. 'You first' defused all conflict and ill feelings. And what we never had didn't make any real difference to us anyway. The memory of our parents and loved ones didn't consist of what they had, but what they meant to us."

When his parents downsized, L. Douglas Coventry, Abiding Hope Lutheran Church, Littleton, Colo., knew the family would have to decide who would get the 1904 player piano — a potential problem between him and his sister. "So at the time I just made sure the piano went to my sister for good rather than become an issue later," he says.

Connie Murphy, Trinity Lutheran Church, Midland, Mich., was the recipient of a similar solution made with her sister, Debi, who is 15 years younger. Their mother told them who was to get what jewelry, with the exception of a big diamond ring. Murphy dreaded the topic because she knew they both wanted it.

"My sister finally brought it up: 'I was thinking about it. I wouldn't get to wear it much with the kind of work I do, so you take it and leave it to me when you die.' A perfect solution! I get to wear the ring during my lifetime and when I'm gone she will have it," Murphy recalls.

Jean Fell, Advent Lutheran Church, Solon, Ohio, went last in her family's turn-taking but says even that worked out. "Being the baby of the family, I certainly didn't think I would be getting a large solitaire of my dreams, and I didn't," she says. "But when the box came my way, my dear grandmother's wedding ring leapt into my heart — much more precious than anything fancier!"

Edward Rondthaler thinks fondly of his wife when he sees her friends, especially those at Our Saviour Lutheran Church, Croton-on-Hudson, N.Y. "After our children made their choices, I felt it appropriate to invite her friends, one at a time, to choose a piece of her jewelry as a remembrance," he says. "It has helped keep a warm memory of her in the hearts of many."

Don't Say "Deserve"

Families frequently devise clever methods of distribution or a code of ethics. Wynne Gillis, Peace Lutheran Church, Belgrade, Mont., tells about a friend who is the oldest of 13 siblings. When her parents died, leaving a farm packed full of possessions, they knew the situation was ripe for trouble. "But they were determined to do it fairly and maintain relationships," Gillis says.

Their first decision was to meet without the complication of spouses but with the help of their pastor. Then they banished the word "deserve" from discussion.

"They determined every sibling would be given an equal share. Period," she says. "The farm would be sold and the proceeds divided equally. Two siblings who had borrowed money from their parents would have that amount deducted from their share."

Edward Rondthaler, 98, was married for 72 years and keeps his wife's memory alive by letting friends choose from her jewelry. Moving from big items to smaller ones, lots were drawn for turns choosing. They could keep, trade or give away.

"Perfect? No. Someone will always grumble. But it was as close to it as I've heard," Gillis says.

Art Feldman's wife, Alice, also comes from a big family — 13 siblings. When her mother died, the old farmhouse was overflowing with "wonderful" stuff, says Feldman, a member of Nazareth Lutheran Church, Withee, Wis. The family decided to divide the treasures by a method modeled after the National Football League's player draft.

They listed the items in each room: the cordless phone in the living room was marked L1, the toaster was K15 and so on. Information was sent out early to ensure perfect attendance, and draft order was determined by drawing names. All agreed the three siblings who had cared for their mom during her final days and had organized the draft would pick one item from the list before the actual draft began, Feldman explains.

The draft went smoothly and was "inspiring to watch," he adds. And just like the NFL, siblings could trade their spot or items and choose items for grandchildren.

"Not one cross word was heard — that day or since," Feldman says. "A deadline for removing the stuff from the house was agreed on. It turned out to be a wonderful day."

Joan Moomey, All Saints Lutheran Church, Toledo, Ohio, tells about their family's sale after her great-grandmother's death at age 92.

An estate dealer priced everything in the house and on Monday of sale week, the nine children and spouses were allowed in the house to buy. The grandchildren shopped the second day, and the great-grandchildren came with their parents and grandparents the third day.

After the public sale, profits were divided among the nine. Those who wanted only money got their wish; those who wanted specific items could buy them, knowing part of the cost was covered by their one-ninth share, she says, adding that "most seemed happy with the arrangement or at least did not argue about it."

"And This Belonged to...."

Several readers are ahead of the game with their earthly goods. Margaret Rubush and her husband, Robert, are both over 80 and each has two children from previous marriages. Rubush says their children and grandchildren aren't aware of everything's origin, so she typed up a list of the more valuable items and included a note: "bookcase, built by Margaret's first husband," "end table, given to us by Bob's mother" or "dining room set purchased by both of us when we lived in Wisconsin."

"When our children or grandchildren come to visit, I tell them to look around and see if there is something they would like to have," says Rubush, a member of Lutheran Church of the Good Shepherd in Seminole, Fla. "If we aren't using it, I give it to them."

Ione Murdock, a member of St. Mark Lutheran Church, Marion, Iowa, is also keenly aware that her sons don't know the value or history of items in her house. She conducted her own Antiques Roadshow with an appraiser who provided a value and general history. Murdock added personal stories and genealogy. "Monetary riches weren't primary," she says. "Family history was a different and valuable kind of wealth to pass on.

"I wrote my sons: 'Enclosed is an inventory of items in our home. Too many families don't talk about inheritance while the parents are alive. I'm doing it now because we're downsizing and because I want us to share family stories. I'd like you to indicate pieces you'd like, either now or later.... History is included without values because I want to know your desires, whether it's [worth] $1 or $3,000.'"

Her sons are now interested in genealogy, and although one son admitted he had no interest in great-grandmother's glassware, he now says, "Anything that has been handled so carefully for more than 100 years should not be trashed."

Even before she was diagnosed with cancer, Bea Favre's mother began wrapping special items and giving them as gifts on birthdays and other special occasions. "It was a meaningful way for the process to begin," says Favre, Lutheran Church of the Good Shepherd, Sacramento, Calif., whose mother died in 1982.

Another frequent rule is: "If you gave it to us, it's yours." Or, this rule established by a family of five brothers who had all been in 4-H and shop classes: "If you made it, you take it."

Finally, Dennis King, Shepherd of the Valley Lutheran Church, Apple Valley, Minn., wrote with a sense of urgency: "Hey, if anyone submits any ideas on how to 'keep the peace' I could sure use them. My siblings are going through this now. I don't understand how property becomes more important than people."

Hey Dennis, this one's for you.

Julie B. Sevig is Section Editor of *The Lutheran*.

19

An Answer for Everything?

John Longhurst

Sometimes you find religion in unusual places, like in the sports section of the newspaper.

That's where ESPN college football analyst Bill Curry was quoted as saying: "A good offense is like a good religion. It should have an answer for everything."

It's a great quote. It's pithy. It's humorous.

It's wrong.

Not about football. Maybe good football offenses really do have answers for everything the opposing team throws at them.

But it's wrong about good religion.

Where did Curry get the idea that religion is about providing answers for everything? From religious people, of course.

In a well-meaning effort to reach out to non-believers, we dumb down faith. We pass out booklets with simple formulas for finding God. We promote books about a prayer that promises to grant our heart's desires. Or we preach the idea that people can be happy, healthy and wealthy if they only believe hard enough.

The result? Instead of attracting thinking non-believers, we repel them. To these people, religion sounds like something for children or for intellectual weaklings — people who need a spiritual crutch to get through life.

Reprinted from the *Mennonite Weekly Review*.

They would likely agree with Sigmund Freud, who likened religion to a "childhood neurosis" that has to be outgrown because "men cannot remain children forever."

Author and social critic Christopher Lasch didn't think religion was just for children. Nor did he believe it existed to provide simple answers to life's most difficult questions.

In a speech in 1991, he said: "What has to be questioned here is the assumption that religion ever provided a set of comprehensive and unambiguous answers to ethical questions, answers completely resistant to skepticism; or that it forestalled speculation about the meaning and purpose of life; or that religious people were unacquainted with existential despair.

In other words, religion isn't just for the intellectually timid. It has room for questions and doubt.

Says author Frederick Buechner: "Whether your faith is that there is a God or that there is not a God, if you don't have any doubts you are either kidding yourself or asleep. Doubts are the ants in the pants of faith. They keep it awake and moving."

In fact, choosing to believe in God today is a more radical and challenging act than deciding not to believe. It's easy to write off God because there is so much suffering in the world, or for any other reason, and then never think about the subject again. Keeping the faith takes a lot more energy and thought.

Philosopher Jonathan Reés, writing about atheism in the winter 2002 issue of Index on Censorship, noted that some of the best critical thinking about our place in the universe was being done by people of faith, not atheists.

At one time, he said, atheism required a rigorous intellect and was a sign of a courageous spirit. Today, however, it "more often than not is the 'do-not-disturb' sign hung out by the intellectually inert," while thoughtful believers are trying to find "appropriate ways of attending to the rough and arbitrary finitude of our existence."

Good religion doesn't try to give us all the answers. Rather, it challenges us on many levels. It especially challenges the idea that we are masters of our fate, and that if we only do, say, sing or pray the right things, God is required to fulfill all our desires.

Is your religion like Bill Curry's good football offense? Does it have an answer for everything? If yes, maybe it's time to ask some hard questions.

John Longhurst is a columnist for the *Winnipeg Free Press* and a member of River East Mennonite Brethren Church in Winnipeg, Manitoba.

20

UMC Panel Condemns Racism at Iliff

Susan Scheib

A review committee from the United Methodist University Senate and General Commission on Religion and Race has put UM-related Iliff School of Theology in Denver on notice: Fix serious problems of institutional racism, or risk losing $900,000 a year in Ministerial Education Funds.

The committee placed Iliff on an immediate "listing with public warning" after a Sept. 27–30, 2004, visit, according to a report released Nov. 2. If there's no significant progress by the time the committee revisits Iliff in six months, the seminary's MEF support — 20 percent of its $5.2-million yearly budget — "will be cut off," said the Rev. J. Philip Wogaman, Iliff's interim president.

According to the report, problems at Iliff center around institutional racism and an "aggressive academic culture and elitism." The Rev. David Maldonado, the denomination's first Hispanic seminary president, told the *Reporter* he was forced to retire in May after four years as president.

The report includes multiple recommendations for improvement, many of which Iliff's board has already put into force, said Dr. Wogaman. Although it's good the committee put some "muscle" behind its report, "we would have implemented these recommendations, even

---

Reprinted from the *United Methodist Reporter*.

without the pressure to do so. They're just good common sense," he said.

Wesley Brown, president of Iliff's board of trustees, said not only will the school cooperate with the report, it asked for the report, and is taking all its recommendations very seriously.

"It's a kick in the pants to make some changes that probably need to be done," he said. "We hear them loud and clear. There are things that need to be fixed, and they can best be fixed by the whole school embracing improvement and change."

Having adopted 20 policy actions responding to review team recommendations, the Iliff board is studying the report in detail to learn more from it, Mr. Brown said. "We have taken the report and distributed various key paragraphs to our various committees, so that the committees carefully study those paragraphs" and report back to the board, which is now meeting once a month, he said.

Meanwhile, the Rev. George E. Tinker, professor of American Indian cultures and religious traditions, said he and the other four faculty of color — comprising 25 percent of Iliff's faculty — are very disturbed at the report. "The report implies the faculty of color... have been intimidated by white faculty," he said.

"Our faculty of color are very strong.... We argue freely and openly with our white colleagues. The freedom to do that is one of the aspects of Iliff that makes it a special school."

Iliff trustees voted Oct. 23 to:

- Ask the General Commission on Religion and Race to help with ongoing racial diversity sensitivity training, revive the school's committee on diversities, and help uncover and remove institutional racism.

- Ask the denomination's Association of Governing Boards to help with trustee training and orientation, as well as change a policy so that a board member not serve simultaneously as the seminary's legal counsel.

- Develop a recruitment/advertising program to reach out to racial/ethnic candidates.
- Give candidates for ordination more preparation in multi-racial cultural settings.
- Hire an ombudsperson and develop a grievance program for the Iliff community.
- Improve the academic culture to ensure respectful hearing of alternate views.
- Revise the faculty handbook.
- Appoint faculty and student board representatives to the board for one-year terms.
- Require that faculty conduct toward students, staffers, administrators and peers — in addition to academic standards — be a criterion for promotion, tenure and appointment to named chairs.
- Develop a communications plan, among other things to emphasize that Dr. Maldonado was not dismissed because of any illegal or immoral activities as president.
- Hire a new dean from outside the institution, after the appointment of a new president.
- Require that the president, as the board's chief executive, may not be excluded from any committee or from access to any relevant documents and that the president is enabled to participate in decisions concerning faculty status.

Governance — one of the key issues in Iliff's troubles — brought about that last resolution, Dr. Wogaman said. The specific problem was exclusion of the president from the faculty committees that hire new professors, promote them, and decide who gets tenure.

At Iliff, Dr. Wogaman said, it had been a longstanding practice that the president was not allowed to participate in those kinds of faculty committees. Iliff's system was "unusual," he said. "I don't know about everybody, but at Wesley Theological Seminary, where I was dean for years, we had nothing like that."

For the president of an institution to be excluded from those committees, even though the president has final veto power, "invites difficulties" and "sets up an adversarial relationship," Dr. Wogaman explained, emphasizing that Iliff's board of trustees has already changed that procedure.

"Now the president is included in the process, which avoids the adversarial relationship at the end of the process. But the board added that the president is expected to show restraint and respect for the faculty's experience, expertise and judgment," he said.

As for how Dr. Maldonado — who stabilized the school's finances and increased its enrollment during his tenure — was treated, and what happened leading to his departure, Dr. Wogaman said, "It's my understanding that when he arrived here, he was greeted with great enthusiasm. But at some point it turned sour.

"The whole thing was very sad. This is a fine school. He's a fine man. Everyone I've met here considered matters in a very positive way — but somehow, the chemistry got messed up. The question was whether President Maldonado's leadership style was different because he is Hispanic, and whether people expected him to be different."

Dr. Wogaman said that part of the problem between Dr. Maldonado and the faculty also may have been a conflict between Iliff's academic standards and other aspects of preparation for pastoral ministry.

Meanwhile, Dr. Maldonado said he is pleased with the committee's findings "and the seriousness with which they took the task."

"I really appreciate what the church has done to investigate, and come to their own conclusions," Dr. Maldonado said. "The bottom line is, if you read the report and connect the dots, you can come to the conclusion that justice has not been done."

The last six months of his time at Iliff, during the winter and spring of 2004, "were very difficult," he said.

"I am deeply disappointed and saddened by what happened, and the way it happened. And I must confess that I do at times experience a 'holy' anger at why this had to occur. But my wife, Charlotte, and I are moving forward. We are grateful that the church has looked into this situation, and we hope that the church will learn from it and that other schools will learn from it, so that others will not have to pay the price that we have paid."

Susan Scheib is a former associate editor of *United Methodist Reporter.*

21

Front-Page News
Thomas C. Willadsen

Recently I read an article asking, "what must the church do to get on the front page of the newspaper?" Typically, churches do not make headlines, and when we do it is because of scandals.

Earlier this year my church got some front-page coverage in *The Oshkosh Northwestern*, so I know the answer to the question about front-page news is "Bury the locally notorious schizophrenic man."

It is, as they say, a long story.

Martin Lloyd was found dead on Wednesday, February 11. A friend of his had left some groceries for him outside his door and after they had sat there a few days, she feared the worst. When the police entered his apartment they called the coroner.

Martin was a peculiar man. When I arrived in Oshkosh five years ago I assumed he was homeless. He looked like Bo Diddley, and acted and smelled like the homeless people I had served while volunteering at a shelter in Chicago. It turned out, though, that he had an apartment and frequented my church. The outgoing interim pastor told me that Martin knew more scripture than anyone else in the congregation and it was true; he had many verses memorized. Often during Adult Sunday School and during less formal worship services he would recite scripture — mostly psalms and epistle passages when he heard a word or phrase that spurred his memory.

When I first spotted Martin at church I assumed that he came just for the food we served at coffee hour. Then I noticed he *never once*

Reprinted from *The Cresset*.

went through the line himself. He would sit off to the side and people would serve him.

"Martin, there are Oreos and chocolate chips today, which would you prefer?"

"Fine, fine."

He also took his coffee "fine, fine."

Martin began to appear at our Wednesday after-school program. He sat on a pew at the edge of the room, just watching. At 5:30, when we make a circle holding hands and sing "Johnny Appleseed" he would stay there, waiting. After a few weeks, we moved the circle to surround Martin, so he would have hands to hold during grace. After a few more weeks the kids were vying for the privileges of holding his hand and filling a plate for him.

It seemed that everyone in town had somehow touched — and been touched by — Martin Lloyd. When I heard of his death I sprang into action. I let the coroner know that we considered Martin a part of our faith community, though he was not officially a member. I let the funeral home know that we would plan a memorial service. We started to track down Martin's next-of-kin.

Martin was 79 years old. He had grown up in Mississippi and had lived and worked in Chicago before coming to Oshkosh. The friend who had left him the groceries thought she knew the name of an aunt somewhere in Mississippi. A member of my church tried to contact the canning factory in Chicago where Martin had worked; I phoned the high school he had attended, but all our leads were pretty lean. After a week, the coroner's office called because Martin's mother had been found, living in St. Louis! She, her daughter, her grandson and his wife and their daughter would all be coming to the memorial service.

Martin was notorious for several reasons. He was often seen fishing at the river. He walked everywhere he went, always with either his fishing gear or his guitar. His trademark, though, was the white construction helmet he wore. All the time. He just felt safer with it.

After his death I learned how proud he was of his background in construction.

He came to Oshkosh about 14 years ago, drawn by the Experimental Aircraft Association's annual convention. A number of people here befriended him. He had a community of people he fished with; people who knew him from his morning coffee at Hardee's; people whom he had lunch with at the Salvation Army; the Presbyterians. If everyone who ever bought him a cheeseburger at Burger King had attended his memorial service our church would have been as full as on Christmas Eve.

Martin liked to travel. Every spring he went to southern California and Mexico for about six weeks. In 2002, he was gone for longer than six weeks. People started to miss him; rumors abounded. *The Northwestern* did an investigation. Martin was found in a nursing home in Los Angeles, having been beaten and robbed. The community worked to bring him back to town. He even got his old apartment back. (Martin lived above a bar, which embarrassed him. Anyone who gave him a ride home had to drop him off a block away, and he would not begin walking home until the driver had driven off.)

Planning the memorial service was a lot like herding cats. We scheduled the service for a Wednesday afternoon, so the after-school kids could attend. Most had never known someone who had died. Since our liturgical dance group practices on Wednesdays, they took part in the service, as did our octogenarian blues harmonica player — every church has one these days — who played a medley of Mississippi delta blues tunes. One of Martin's friends prepared a ten page astrological reading for me. While I do not understand the significance of zodiacal cusps, I was amazed to learn that people with Martin's birthday are expected to be wanderers who find it difficult to settle any place and often drift from job to job. Still, I found myself unable to use these insights in my homily.

Two of Martin's fishing buddies paid for his obituary. Employees from a printer who often had lunch with Martin contributed the bulletins. Someone else brought the flowers. We stretched our Lenten

Simple Supper Chili Feed and invited members to bring salads and dessert for the luncheon following the service. It wasn't the miracle of loaves and fishes, but there was plenty of food for everyone.

In addition to the front-page coverage of the service, several things were especially gratifying to me. I am very proud that the congregation I serve and this community had been able to care for one of our vulnerable people. Throughout the days leading up to the service the line "guard each man's dignity and save each man's pride" from "We Are One in the Spirit" kept echoing in my head.

I think Martin's family did not realize how precious Martin was to Oshkosh. They marveled at the kindness that was shown to one his sister knew as "a very eccentric young man."

Finally, memorial money poured in to the church. Typically we have a formula which divides memorials several ways, but in Martin's case the congregation's ruling board decided to have all the memorial money go toward purchasing a burial marker which features a man fishing and a guitar and reads

> Martin Lloyd
> 1924–2004
> A Gentle Giant

The remaining money is in a fund that aids travelers stranded in Oshkosh. Now we are able to help anyone in a situation like Martin's in Los Angeles.

Martin Lloyd's death and memorial service were indeed front-page news in this town of 60,000. But every day, without the headlines, churches extend kindness, compassion, respect, and grace to eccentric, vulnerable people. And find themselves blessed when a Martin Lloyd comes along.

Thomas C. Willadsen is the pastor at the First Presbyterian Church in Oshkosh, Wisconsin.

22

"King of Pop" More Like a "God"
Our Adulation for Michael Jackson Unstinting
David W. Reid

While the facts in the criminal case against Michael Jackson have yet to be tried in court, the fantasy life of Neverland Ranch presents a clear indictment of America's cultural idolatry, said a scholar who studies religion and culture at Iliff School of Theology in Denver.

"One way to think and talk about this theologically is to talk about the way in which our cultural celebrities become gods," said Jeffrey H. Mahan, professor of ministry, media and culture at the United Methodist seminary. "We treat them in that way. We are fascinated with them. We give their lives a level of meaning that is expanded and beyond the human."

The public projects this image onto celebrities, but the celebrities also encourage it, he said.

"We know that [Jackson] has embraced a bizarre fascination with childhood so that he has taken on this kind of childlike self-identity — the voice, the costuming, the fascination with toys and play, with the need to surround himself with children," said Mahan. In addition, he said, Jackson has a history of relationships with children that appear to be sex-laden.

The theological implications point to "not just his idolatry, but our own cultural idolatry," said Mahan. "Once you frame it that way, then what you have is the sacrifice of the children to the god."

Reprinted from *Vital Theology*.

Parents bring their children to Neverland Ranch to experience the divine, if only for a short time, said Mahan, who is co-editor of the book *Religion and Popular Culture in America*.

"To be close to the god, one appeases the god, one makes offerings to the god, one sacrifices to the god. And clearly people have sacrificed their children to this god. Whether he is in fact a child molester or not, to allow young children to be unsupervised in the presence of any adult the family doesn't know well — but certainly an adult about whom there have been significant public charges and questions — seems just bizarre. One can't imagine that these parents would make these choices for the strange man down the street."

In December, 2003, prosecutors charged Jackson with seven counts of child molestation, accusing the 45-year-old King of Pop of having "substantial sexual conduct" with a boy under 14 in February and March. His accuser is a cancer-stricken boy who appeared with Jackson in a documentary in February. Jackson also faces two counts of administering an intoxicating agent for the purpose of committing a felony.

"I think it is helpful to begin to say that celebrities become the gods of this culture," said Mahan, "and particularly when they are the gods of a consumer culture in which appearance is everything, possession of things is everything, and so to be rich, to be famous is the cultural goal."

Jackson's defense attorney Mark Geragos presents a different view of the ranch and its visitors.

On Dec. 18, he told CNN's Larry King: "You have to see this Neverland facility. This place. It is wonderful. It's idyllic. It is 2,700 acres... nestled in the mountains up there. It's got an amusement park, it's got a miniature Disneyland train station there with the train that goes around. It's got a lake with swans in it. People come up — he opens his doors, busloads of disadvantaged people and it's the most exciting thing in the world to them."

To become a god also requires immortality, Mahan noted, and the denial of death has surrounded Jackson since 1986 when the *National*

Enquirer published a photo of him in a hyperbaric oxygen chamber designed to extend his lifespan.

While a series of surgeries have made Jackson appear more and more white, these operations have also allowed a man in his mid-40s to present himself as a hairless adolescent who is resistant to aging.

Jackson's brother, Jermaine, recently conceded to Larry King that his brother is "child-like," but Mahan believes that "childish" is a more accurate term and that the star's self-identity "is in part about having no limits."

The "little-boy-innocence voice" is a denial of the possibility of Jackson's own death, said Mahan, who is also an ordained clergyman in the United Methodist Church. The financial debt that Jackson carries and the $30 million that was spent producing his latest CD are additional indications of his denial of limits, he said.

The denial of limits also "brings you to the possibility of sexual interaction with children," said Mahan.

"For somebody who has no limits, who is unwilling to hear the counsel of others where there ought to be boundaries and limits in life, all kinds of sexual transgressions become possible," he said.

Indeed, sexual activity was evidence of the power of ancient gods. Such gods were unfaithful to their wives when married, came down to earth to have sex with mortals, crossed over traditional boundaries about available sex partners, and proved their godliness by suffering no consequences.

But when certain lines are crossed, the broader culture invokes its own boundaries on our contemporary gods, said Mahan.

"They turn on the celebrity," he said.

The cultural attack on the celebrity starts "when we begin to be kind of too aware of all of this and begin to say, 'no, no, that's not appropriate. We don't want to participate in that.' We want to deny our participation in it and make the celebrity entirely the villain."

Think of pioneer film star Fatty Arbuckle, said Mahan. He was paid the unheard-of salary of $1 million and given unlimited artistic freedom. But when he was charged in the death of a young actress in 1921, his audience retreated in horror.

Distancing ourselves from fallen celebrities is a way to maintain our own sense of moral superiority, said Mahan. We tell ourselves that we could be that celebrity, but we have made better moral choices.

"I am allowed to be fascinated for a period with somebody like Michael Jackson, to see what it would be like to simply live on an estate like Neverland, to be able to fulfill any fantasy that you have, to perpetuate this child-like identity, to be admired around the world," he said. "And then I'm allowed to step back and say, 'Oh, these transgressions. I would never do that. And in fact the reason I'm not successful and famous and wealthy is because I have made superior moral choices.'"

Mahan said that tensions about celebrity and our cultural ambivalence toward success come together in such stories. On the one hand, we hold fast to the American dream that anybody can be successful, that anybody can be president or be Michael Jackson. On the other hand, we wonder why this has not happened to us or to our children.

Lastly, Mahan draws parallels between celebrities imbued with god-like qualities and the biblical story of Abraham and Isaac. Abraham offers up his child to be consumed by God. But the biblical story says that ultimately God does not require that of us and that God provides a ram so the child does not have to be sacrificed.

"The tragedy about making Michael Jackson a god," said Mahan, "is that then the child has to be consumed."

David W. Reid is the editor of *Vital Theology*.

23

Eager for Education
Marla Pierson Lester

Wind sweeps through the missing windowpanes and rustles papers in Annie Haluciso's first grade classroom in Zambia's Southern Province. The students sit attentively on the floor, awaiting their teacher's next move.

She pulls out a drawing of a chicken. Enthusiasm erupts and hands shoot up. Each child is eager to be the one who identifies the *nkuku*, the local Tonga word for chicken.

Like other rural schools in Zambia — and indeed some urban ones — Hamoonde Basic School's rooms have few windowpanes to block the elements. Doors are missing, desks are inadequate and books are scarce. Yet those inside are the fortunate ones.

For every child vying to identify the *nkuku*, there are many who were not accepted into first grade. Hamoonde's first grade has space for 40 children; each year the school has an average of 120 applicants for those spots.

Most Zambian children receive a substandard level of education, despite government attempts to improve the quality and availability of schooling. Primary schools and schools in rural areas such as Hamoonde teach two different groupings of children each day in classes that sometimes top 50 students. Yet there are still not enough schools to accommodate every child. Estimates indicate that perhaps fewer than 40 percent of school-age children ever find a place in the formal educational system.

Reprinted from *A Common Place*.

Overcrowding is only one of many obstacles. National factors such as the HIV/AIDS epidemic and low teachers' salaries impact schooling. Insufficient harvests — and the hunger that brings — can virtually empty classrooms. Even in a good year, attendance depends on a family's circumstances.

The gaps that seem woven into the educational experience in Zambia can mean more than a blank spot in a teacher's attendance book. The system is built on the one British colonizers brought to Zambia. Classwork must prepare students for standardized tests that are required if students are to progress beyond seventh, ninth and 12th grades. Absences, and any gaps in the material learned, can determine whether a child will pass.

No matter the odds, parents who may have little formal schooling themselves are determined to provide their children with an education. They haul piles of stones, make bricks or construct latrines to help out the school. They sell chickens to pay for their children's school fees or uniforms.

Teachers enter their ill-equipped classrooms each day, ready to lead their classes despite shortages of books and even desks.

In this context, MCC's Global Family Program — administered through Zambian Brethren in Christ (BIC) church schools — offers welcome measures of encouragement to parents and school officials in their quest to help children learn.

Education has always been a priority for MCC's work in Zambia, which began in 1962 with North American volunteers coming to teach in Zambian schools through the Teachers Abroad (TAP) program. Assignments were through the BIC church, still MCC's primary partner in Zambia.

Hamoonde lies near the heart of BIC missions in Zambia. In 1906, the first BIC missionary in the country, Frances Davidson, came to nearby Macha, crossing the Zambezi River into what was then Northern Rhodesia. Among other ministries, she established a school, an education tradition that continues in the Zambian BIC churches. Today, there are some 154 BIC congregations in Zambia with more than 15,000 members; the church elected its first national bishop in 1978.

Hamoonde, like other Zambian BIC schools, is known as a grant-assisted school. Teachers are posted and paid by Zambia's Ministry of Education. The BIC church, through its Educational Administrative Committee and education secretary, is responsible for administration and can select teachers for management positions. The church can also request that certain qualified teachers, such as BIC church members, be posted to its schools.

At Hamoonde, needs far outstrip what the government provides. Jennipher Mulongo, second and fourth grade teacher, hauls in the day's teaching materials. Her classroom has no door so she knows that any pictures or books she leaves behind may well be taken. At her home, provided by the school, she blocks broken windows as best she can and waits on repairs to the doorknob that must now be pried open with a spoon.

Funds from Global Family, MCC's sponsorship and education program, help fill the gaps. North American sponsors each contribute $22 Cdn./$17 U.S. monthly. The funds buy uniforms, sweaters, exercise books, extra pens and pencils. Hamoonde school officials also use some money for teacher housing and medical aid for students, such as those injured in a fire several years ago.

"I feel more like the fellow pupils," said seventh-grade student Kenneth Dubeka, who received a uniform and sweater. "I used to feel out of place sometimes."

Instead of four exercise books, he has 12 — a crucial stockpile in a system where copying problems and passages is the mode of education. Kenneth had long needed school supplies. But he wasn't eligible for assistance until after his mother died last year. At Hamoonde, students who have lost one or more parents have first priority in the extensive demand for aid.

Kenneth, when asked how long he will stay in school, says ninth grade — the time his older brothers left school. But even going to eighth grade requires that he pass exams that stumped 37 of the 55

Hamoonde students who took them in 2002. In the upper grades, school fees are also required. Kenneth's father, Joseph Dubeka, says Kenneth may go as far in school as he likes. But he doesn't know how he would pay for it. His health is failing, his legs weak and stomach ill.

Family circumstance is often a determining factor in how much education a child will receive in Zambia. Teachers have learned that children who do not have warm clothing, for instance, will not come to class in chilly weather. Children without enough exercise books may skip school to preserve the blank pages. Illnesses, particularly malaria, often cause students to miss school.

But with the HIV/AIDS crisis, the difficulties are magnified enormously. Today, as many as one in five adults in Zambia is infected with HIV, the virus that causes AIDS. Increasingly, orphans are coming to live with relatives. In impoverished, rural areas, these expanded families struggle to find the money to pay for orphans' school expenses.

HIV/AIDS has also exacerbated the nationwide teacher shortage. A few years ago, Hamoonde had only two to three teachers for grades 1 through 7. The government required classes be run according to schedule. They did, albeit with teachers responsible for more than one class at a time.

"When you are teaching two or three classes, you are only there to pretend to teach them — only to keep them busy," said head teacher Gilbert Muzyamba.

In 2001, the health department closed the school down until new latrines could be constructed — another disruption to children's learning.

When the 2002 harvest of maize, the area's staple crop, failed, many students were too weak to walk to school. Others spent days with their parents, searching for something edible in the bush.

Mulongo, the second and fourth grade teacher, remembers how those who did attend would remain quiet at break. She points to the active children on the playground as a sign times are surely better. Teachers and students are looking forward.

On breaks, students help clean the school or haul water. In class they lean forward, nestled together on crowded benches, listening intently and training their tongues to handle the unfamiliar sounds of English, the language required for their classwork. They pore over exercise books, copying passages and problems from the board and compete to be the first to answer a question.

Older students at Hamoonde must already know their future schooling hinges on far more than their enthusiasm and knowledge. Yet even in later grades, a teacher's question may well turn the class into a sea of waving arms, of eager pupils reaching for a better life the best way they know how — through education.

Marla Pierson Lester is a Mennonite Central Committee writer.

24

Pottery-Making Rare in State Baptist Churches

Sandra Bearden

Pottery proves time and time again that it is one of the oldest and most enduring of the arts.

Archaeologists continue to unearth remains of jars and pots thousands of years old, and the walls of ancient Egyptian tombs show potters at work.

More than 600 years before Christ, Jeremiah carried this message from God to the people of Israel: "As the clay is in the potter's hand, so are you in My hand" (Jer. 18:6).

However, evidence of this ancient art form is rare in the programs or fine arts conservatories of Alabama Baptist churches.

Keith Hibbs, who oversees creative arts ministries for the Alabama Baptist State Board of Missions, said a few churches offer painting classes. However, he knows of none teaching pottery courses.

"The level of difficulty may be the main reason [pottery classes aren't offered]," Hibbs said.

In addition to the aesthetic aspect of pottery making, the potter must form vessels from balls or coils of clay using a manually or electrically operated potter's wheel.

After "throwing" the pot, the artisan permanently hardens it by firing vessels in a kiln. The potter can then decorate the object, either by dipping it into a glaze or by painting on designs.

Reprinted from *The Alabama Baptist*.

On the other hand, ceramics classes are common in many churches. Ceramics, which means "potter's clay," also involves the use of clay, other materials and a kiln.

But students normally use preformed molds to make decorative or practical objects such as Christmas angels, vases and ornaments.

"I can tell many stories of how our ceramics program is used to minister to the sick and homebound," said Susan Forehand, director of women's ministries at Shades Mountain Baptist Church, Vestavia Hills, in Birmingham Association.

While pottery-making may not play a role in Alabama Baptist church programs, some artists use pottery in presentations at church or denominational meetings.

For example, potters sometimes help Margaret Kennedy of Dothan, a writer and public speaker, in presenting a program called "In These Jars of Clay."

Kennedy said the presentation demonstrates the purpose God has for individuals.

"My theme addresses why God would deposit His greatest treasure — Christ — in unfit vessels (humanity)," she said.

"I have a potter demonstrating his or her work, with displays of earthen vessels in the background," she said. "I encourage people that no matter what kind of pot you are — sturdy and practical, or fine and fragile — God has a purpose in your life.

"We also use broken pieces of pottery to represent whatever people are holding onto that prevents complete dedication to Christ," Kennedy said. "In an invitation, those broken pieces are surrendered."

Stephen Glaze, former Judson College art professor now on the faculty of Mississippi College, teams with his artist wife, Ruth, to present art devotionals at churches.

"When we first started this ministry, I was working on a doctoral program at Florida State University and teaching at Judson," Glaze said.

"Part of my dissertation dealt with the attitudes of Southern Baptists toward art in the church," he said. "I worked in six Alabama churches, testing attitudes, conducting workshops and presenting devotionals using art activities.

"I then post-tested attitudes. What I found was that Baptists haven't been very receptive to the arts," Glaze said.

"But if you can show that art enhances spiritual growth in fellow believers and that it's something that edifies the heart, attitudes change," he said.

Glaze said the couple's devotionals feature combinations of painting, pottery, sculpture and music.

These accompany written and spoken Scripture passages. He often uses a verse from Jeremiah as a key Scripture.

"When you combine all these media, people will remember what they see and hear for many years," Glaze said.

"People have come up to me 10 or 15 years after they've seen one of those pottery devotionals and tell me what I did and the spiritual points I made," he said. "I use art as a symbol of something beyond it.

"Just as Jesus spoke in parables so that people would better understand His meaning, I believe He also took advantage of visuals as He spoke," Glaze said.

Sandra Bearden is a correspondent for *The Alabama Baptist*.

25

How Blind I Was

Sharon Sheridan

It took becoming a parent for me to realize there was more to McVickar than I ever suspected.

His name was McVickar.

He sat near the front of the church on the Epistle side and, for a number of months, regular as Christmas, rose from his seat each Sunday during the sermon to visit the lavatory. He'd pause in the middle of the nave, bow to the altar, then continue past the preacher with stilted gait, arms swinging, toward the side door. A few minutes later, he'd reverse the process.

His teeth were a little crooked. They showed often in a smile.

McVickar regularly attended the morning Adult Forum, regardless of the topic, and never missed coffee hour. He'd approach familiar parishioners, perhaps with a cup of coffee tipping toward disaster, maybe with a few crumbs on his chin, usually with an insistent question or comment. These, too, were predictable: *Where is priest so-and-so? Is it time for service? Such-and-such a former staff member now is at X location.*

I learned to acknowledge the question or comment quickly, then turn back to my conversation with someone else.

McVickar was, in today's lingo, developmentally disabled. Over the years, he lived with family and in various institutions in the area and attended St. Peter's Episcopal Church with a devotion few could

---

Reprinted from *Episcopal Life*.

match. I suspect many people, however, credited that regularity more with routine than with faith.

It took becoming a parent for me to realize there was more to McVickar than I ever suspected.

I often had heard how we become full members of the church from the moment of baptism. A nice sentiment, I thought, but what can a baby offer?

After my son was born, I learned the answer quickly. He offered "smile ministry." He cheered people up. People I never talked with before approached and initiated conversations about — and with — my child.

That included McVickar.

For some reason, McVickar and my son bonded. McVickar wanted to know how he was, when his birthday was, where he lived, what he liked to eat. He expressed great concern if his little buddy was home ill and inquired about his health regularly even after he returned to church.

McVickar understood the strain of behaving properly in church. My son's in-the-pew antics, which frustrated and embarrassed me, amused McVickar immensely.

Suddenly, McVickar knew my name. As mother of my son, I had become a more important person to him.

As I discovered how observant and "on-the-ball" McVickar was, he became a more important person to me, too, although I sometimes had trouble understanding his speech.

I learned a bit about his life, his likes and dislikes. I listened to stories, followed with a smile and his favorite phrase, "I'n't that something?"

A few weeks ago, I met our soon-to-be-interim rector. He commented about using written sermons to avoid being distracted by congregants.

"Wait till he meets McVickar!" someone said.

Sadly, he never had the chance. McVickar entered the hospital shortly after Halloween and died at age 71 on Jan. 10.

Since his funeral, I find myself remembering Jesus' statements about becoming like little children to enter heaven. And I think about what McVickar taught me about respecting the dignity of every human being.

I learned early on not to take children for granted. I remember a parent telling me his children liked me as a baby sitter because I treated them like "little people." And I remember watching my niece at age one and a half and thinking, "Wow, kids really understand more than a lot of people give them credit for."

But, perhaps because I prize intellectual pursuits, I suspect I didn't grant full respect to the developmentally disabled. For a long time, I discounted McVickar's true worth.

Now, I remember Harlem watchmaker and evangelist Corrie ten Boom's statement to a Nazi interrogator that the retarded people she cared for "may be worth more than a watchmaker — or a lieutenant."

Before his death, the clergy administering last rites to McVickar thought he wasn't conscious of their presence — until they reached the Lord's Prayer. He turned and began mouthing the familiar words through the oxygen mask.

In a world of theological bickering and impassioned protests about who's in and who's out of the church, McVickar simply lived as a child of God and accepted everyone else as God's child, too. He lived a life of faith and remained faithful unto death.

I'n't that something?

Sharon Sheridan, freelance writer and editor, lives in Flanders, New Jersey, and attends St. Peter's Episcopal Church in Morristown.

26

Q&A

James Ayers

Q: *I recently asked about putting flowers on the altar, and our minister became quite upset. He insisted we do not have an altar in the church, we have a Communion table. Why was this such a big deal to him?*

A: An altar is usually made of solid stone, and animals are sacrificed and burned there (Genesis 8:20, Leviticus 1:1–9). A table is a flat surface, commonly wood, the kind of place where people sit to eat a meal.

During the celebration of the Eucharist, what does the officiant do? That question formed part of the polemic of the Reformation. The early Presbyterians (among others) understood that in the Roman mass the priest offers the body of Jesus as a sacrifice to God, on the church altar right now. They rejected this idea, and insisted that Jesus had offered himself as sacrifice once for all, at one unrepeatable moment of history. So Presbyterians say the Lord's Supper is a meal served at a table, where we are spiritually fed by Jesus with these symbols of his life given for us.

Our heritage teaches us to call the piece of furniture at the front of the chancel a table rather than an altar.

Except sometimes we don't. People often speak colloquially. That is what you did. You probably were not looking for a theology lesson; you just wanted to know where to put the flowers. Your

---

Reprinted from *Presbyterians Today*.

minister might have perceived that, and saved the history lesson for another time.

Q: *Why don't Presbyterians have altar calls?*

A: Hmmm. Because we don't have altars? No, that can't be it. The altar rail and the altar call are common parts of religious life among many American denominations that are quite clear that they have no altar on which they offer sacrifices to God.

An altar call is a time when individuals come forward, kneel at the altar rail, and pray: to receive Christ as their Savior, or to dedicate their life to Christian service. This can be a powerful moment in which people experience God's call with special clarity.

Many Presbyterians get quite squeamish about this, however. A good reason might be this: We must learn to confess and repent and walk as Christians throughout our lives. We must not teach ourselves that we only need to do this once, when we come forward at an altar call.

But the most common reason is probably that we feel embarrassed about people experiencing that depth of emotion and dedication within a worship service.

James Ayers, a Presbyterian minister, writer, and speaker, is a member-at-large of Southern Kansas Presbytery.

27

Why It Was Impossible for Us to Sign Declaration

Leanne Larmondin

A handful of readers have written to *Anglican Journal* about our decision not to cover the recent gathering of Essentials in Ottawa due to the organization's requirement that participants (including media) sign a declaration of faith that included the phrase "adultery, fornication and homosexual unions are intimacies contrary to God's design."

They were also asked to sign a "statement of repudiation and disassociation from the actions of the General Synod" on the matter of same-sex relationships.

(In fact, organizers of the gathering gave mixed messages to interested journalists. They initially stated that the conference was closed to media so that, in the words of one organizer, "anyone can express themselves and can feel safe and so there is editorial control." Later, they said media who signed the declaration of faith and the other statement would be permitted to attend the conference.)

Readers have asked why it was that *Anglican Journal* could not find an "orthodox" staff writer to cover the gathering on Essentials' terms.

The answer is simple: the issue is not about orthodoxy. It never was.

Professional journalists do not publicly endorse the beliefs of a group they are supposed to be covering objectively. For that reason,

---

Reprinted from *The Anglican Journal*.

Why It Was Impossible for Us to Sign Declaration

you will not find a *Journal* reporter wearing a rainbow Integrity sticker at General Synod or signing the petition of a conservative group. Think for a moment how your opinion of the news would change if a television news anchor were to read the news with a Liberal party button on her lapel. If we as journalists compromise our integrity, we damage the trust our readers have in our newspaper. The editorial staff of *Anglican Journal* takes this responsibility very seriously.

Additionally, it should be noted that no other group in the church — not the house of bishops, the Council of General Synod, Fidelity, Integrity or Anglican Church Women — determines how it is to be covered by the *Journal*. That is because the Anglican Church of Canada — which is recognized throughout the Anglican Communion as one of the most transparent of all the churches — long ago decided that it is valuable to have a free, independent press. This is a relative rarity, both in the wider Anglican Communion and many other denominations.

The *Journal*'s editorial independence is perhaps well known in some church circles, but it is often misunderstood. Put simply, it is predicated on the belief that there is value to the church in having a national publication, accessible to the greatest number of constituents possible, that stands back from the church to examine critically what it does and does not do and how it does or does not do it. (Full disclosure: that thought is from Vianney Carriere, the national church's director of communications and information resources. He made the point when he was the editor of *Anglican Journal*.)

There is also a practical reason why *Anglican Journal* remains editorially independent. The *Journal* receives substantial funding from Heritage Canada, a federal government department which subsidizes mailing costs for Canadian periodicals. Heritage policy is clear that any publication would be rendered ineligible for postal subsidies if it were to be "published directly or indirectly by such groups and organizations as ... religious ... organizations, and primarily report on the activities of the group or organization, or primarily promote the interests of the group or organization or its members."

Currently, for instance, *Anglican Journal* is mailed at an average cost of $0.14 per copy; without the Heritage Canada subsidy, that cost would rise to at least $0.56 — four times the subsidized cost. Total mailing costs each year are more than $300,000; without subsidies, that total would top $1.2 million. So, if *Anglican Journal*'s independent editorial policy were abandoned, we would lose the postal subsidies that make possible the production and distribution of *Anglican Journal* and the diocesan newspapers (which are printed and mailed together with the Journal).

From time to time, readers suggest that certain stories should not be covered in the *Journal* because they show the church in a bad light. Some readers do not expect to read bad news in a church newspaper. Others write to the newspaper asking (and sometimes demanding) that we cease our coverage of issues that they find troubling. But religious journalism and church newspapers should not be held to a different standard than secular media. Ignoring an issue because it causes discomfort or even outrage for some readers is disingenuous.

Our mandate is to cover the Anglican Church of Canada in all of its complexity, from the knitting ministries to the residential school settlement; from the parish fundraising projects to the financial scandals; from the healing programs to the cases of sexual misconduct.

The independent editorial policy is in place to serve you, the reader.

Leanne Larmondin is the editor of the *Anglican Journal*.

28

Finding the Way Home

Ingrid Christiansen

All this Jesus said to the crowd in parables: indeed, he said nothing to them without a parable. (Matthew 13:34)

It was the paths that got them. Ordinary paths through the woods, going here and there — to a waterfall, to a garden, into the mountains, past lakes, even across the mountains to the other side. The paths became parables to them, and like all parables, the meaning of the parables grew and grew. On the first day they wondered, *"How can you tell what is a path, and what is just dirt on the forest floor?"*

Who are these women who could not see paths? For a number of years, women recovering from prostitution at Genesis House in Chicago have gone on a spiritual retreat to Holden Village, the Lutheran retreat center in the Cascade Mountains. Many of them have never been outside the city limits of Chicago — almost none of them have been on an airplane, or seen a mountain, a forest, or even a lake although Chicago's entire eastern boundary is Lake Michigan. When you are poor and abused, you stay on familiar turf, and that turf is where the streets are rough, and life is marked by the crack house on the block, the shiny cars with suburban license plates on the corner, and a dingy apartment with too many kids in it. Going for a week into the wilderness is almost unfathomable. But go they do.

Reprinted from *Lutheran Woman Today*.

Where the Path Begins

The trip begins well before the trip, of course. At Genesis House, the residential treatment home where they are living, we talk together about clothes: what are appropriate clothes to wear on an airplane, in restaurants in Washington state, and most importantly, high up in the Cascade Mountains. Women who have worked the streets of Chicago for years as prostitutes have only a vague sense of what would be appropriate clothes. That is one of the many skills they gain while spending a year in recovery from sex work. What *are* gym shoes, windbreakers?

In pre-trip preparation we also talk about fear: What will you do if you get lost in the airport in Chicago or in Seattle? The biggest fear these women have about going to the mountains is the fear of getting lost *in the woods* at Holden. Women who have no fear on the most dangerous streets in Chicago are tremendously afraid of losing their way in settings where many of us are confident. We talk together about bears, wolves, mosquitoes.

That they honestly have a hard time seeing a path through the woods is hard for us to understand. This teaches us — their "teachers" — a great deal about point of view, about seeing as a cultural experience. We began to wonder what our guests can see that we cannot.

It is easy to begin an experience such as this seeing too many we/they dichotomies. Interestingly to me, one who has taught at Holden many times and thrice directed their summer program, the women have no fear of *us* — the guests, staff, and teachers, Lutherans from Minnesota and Washington, from North Dakota and Pennsylvania, who inhabit Holden Village all summer. I'm not sure the same could be said of many of us, that we would not harbor a fear of these women whose lives have been so different from many of ours. One goal is to find common ground, mutual respect, and understanding. And even Christian community and some love.

Traveling Companions

Once I was working with a Holden staff member preparing for the Genesis House women to arrive, and she asked me: "Are these prostitutes Christian?" I told her what one very broken, addicted woman working in prostitution once told me: She said, "Ingrid, I wouldn't still *be* here, if Jesus didn't love me."

Because the women are all in recovery for addiction and prostitution, their days at Holden are very structured. The Genesis House staff who accompany them make a detailed plan for each day of each participant. The women reside alongside the other guests, scattered among various lodges. They attend all the same sessions every other guest attends. When they are in Bible study, which is a popular early-morning class, they bring the stories of their lives to the discussion, just as all of the rest of us do in Bible study. We use the words of the Bible to illuminate our lives in ways that will gives us relief from hurt, hope and focus for the future, and a sense of grace and forgiveness.

One day, Bishop Steve Ullestead from Iowa was leading the Bible study. A story he was working on involved the gates around a city. The Genesis House women immediately related to the idea of being barred from the central city, of being an outsider, not acceptable in the eyes of the public or of God. Their path stops at the gate, and they desperately want in. Other guests related their fear and avoidance of cities, and much laughter ensued at the differences in point of view.

As the Bible study neared its end, Bishop Ullestead had the group looking for the love and forgiveness of God in the story. One of the Genesis House women began to cry. She said her sins were too great, that she could not be forgiven. I was leaning over the edge of the balcony, just above the woman who had spoken so heartbreakingly about her sins. As I watched, an older woman from the prairie reached out and touched her shoulder. She whispered in a clearly audible whisper, "My sins are also great; I need to work on forgiving myself, too. Could we go for a walk after class?" Off they went after class, arm in arm, providing the comfort and solace of one Christian to another, down a new path for them both.

Overcoming Roadblocks

Hiking is a big activity at Holden. Although our friends from Genesis House are called streetwalkers, hiking, indeed exercise of any sort, is not a big activity in their former way of life. While these women are in residence at Holden, they are required by their staff to do four things each day: attend Bible study, volunteer in a Holden work area, attend daily worship, and take a significant walk or hike. The goal of the hiking requirement is for them to be ready by week's end to hike to Hart Lake, four miles up into the Railroad Creek valley. On the big day, they are full of trepidation. Each woman is concerned: Can I make it to Hart Lake? What will we find out there in the mountains, so far from this little village? What if we get lost? We don't know the way, we can't find the path.

Halfway to Hart Lake the path crosses a fast-flowing mountain stream, cold, deep, and ferocious looking; a narrow bridge with no railings goes over it. On a recent hike, when we arrived at the stream and took out our morning snack, one woman, Kendra, began crying. She said she is afraid of heights, afraid of bridges, and afraid of water. She said she would have to go back, and she was afraid of going back alone, but she simply could not go on. The staff all looked worriedly at one another. Kendra was the least popular of the residents, and the staff were not surprised that she would "pull this stunt." As they talked among themselves about sending one staff member back with Kendra, the Genesis House residents sat down in a circle, held hands, and began to pray. After fervent prayer, they said to Kendra, we are going to go across that bridge holding hands, together. If one of us falls, we all fall. But we are not going anywhere without you. And they didn't.

Finding the Way Home 145

That evening, in their reflection session, they were jubilant. They had all made it, including Sasha, who had severe asthma. But what pleased them the most was Kendra's triumph over her fears, and the triumph of the group over the divisiveness that Kendra had been representing until they all pulled together to help her over an enormous obstacle. It was at that point that the path had cleared, and they could continue on toward the goal.

The Road to Recovery

In one of the group's many discussions about paths, they began to realize that a path is a good metaphor for what they were going through in their recovery. They talked about how others had gone before, especially in AA and NA, and with the 12 steps had worn a path open for them. All they had to do was pay attention to those 12 steps and the way would be clear.

The next day, the group began to talk of Jesus as the maker of the path. They discussed how Jesus had worn a path clear for them, how they had only to look to the parables in the Bible to discern the way. Another day, as they spoke of avoiding bad influences, they noticed that there are many paths open to all of us. The important part is to be sure the path we choose has been worn by the right feet, the feet of the One we want to follow. When one woman spoke of huge obstacles in her path, they remembered the courage and prayer needed to cross the stream. They decided you did not need to abandon a path just because you encountered an obstacle on it.

As the parable of the paths grew, so did the distance we could hike on paths. We all grew in our faith, and the heart of Holden Village grew. The days at Holden are always rich, full of story and joy. It is no wonder, then, that other guests often come up to the staff from Genesis House and ask, "Which Bible study are the women going to tomorrow, because I want to go to that one. Their stories enrich the class so much." And we are all reminded again that we share the paths on which we walk, and the gifts along the way are many and great.

Ingrid Christiansen worked as a professor of urban studies in Chicago for thirty years and now serves as a sentencing advocate for people facing the death penalty. She and her husband, John Kretzmann, are members of Ebenezer Lutheran Church in Chicago. This article was provided by *Lutheran Woman Today*, the magazine of the Women of the Evangelical Lutheran Church in America.

29

CBS, NBC Refuse to Air Church's Television Advertisement

United Church of Christ Ad Highlighting Jesus' Extravagant Welcome Called "Too Controversial"

J. Bennett Guess

The CBS and NBC television networks are refusing to run a 30-second television ad from the United Church of Christ because its all-inclusive welcome has been deemed "too controversial."

The ad, part of the denomination's new, broad identity campaign set to begin airing nationwide on Dec. 1, 2004, states that — like Jesus — the United Church of Christ (UCC) seeks to welcome all people, regardless of ability, age, race, economic circumstance or sexual orientation.

According to a written explanation from CBS, the UCC is being denied network access because its ad implies acceptance of gay and lesbian couples — among other minority constituencies.

"Because this commercial touches on the exclusion of gay couples and other minority groups by other individuals and organizations," reads an explanation from CBS, "and the fact the Executive Branch has recently proposed a Constitutional Amendment to define marriage as a union between a man and a woman, this spot is unacceptable for broadcast on the [CBS and UPN] networks."

Similarly, a rejection by NBC declared the spot "too controversial."

Reprinted from *United Church News*.

"It's ironic that after a political season awash in commercials based on fear and deception by both parties seen on all the major networks, an ad with a message of welcome and inclusion would be deemed too controversial," says the Rev. John H. Thomas, the UCC's general minister and president. "What's going on here?"

Negotiations between network officials and the church's representatives broke down on Nov. 30, the day before the ad campaign begins airing nationwide on a combination of broadcast and cable networks. The ad has been accepted and will air on a number of networks, including ABC Family, AMC, BET, Discovery, Fox, Hallmark, History, Nick@Nite, TBS, TNT, Travel and TV Land, among others.

The debut thirty-second commercial features two muscle-bound "bouncers" standing guard outside a symbolic, picturesque church and selecting which persons are permitted to attend Sunday services. Written text interrupts the scene, announcing, "Jesus didn't turn people away. Neither do we." A narrator then proclaims the UCC's commitment to Jesus' extravagant welcome: "No matter who you are, or where you are on life's journey, you are welcome here." (The ad can be viewed online at *stillspeaking.com*.)

In focus groups and test market research conducted before the campaign's national rollout, the UCC found that many people throughout the country feel alienated by churches. The television ad is geared toward those persons who, for whatever reason, have not felt welcomed or comfortable in a church.

"We find it disturbing that the networks in question seem to have no problem exploiting gay persons through mindless comedies or titillating dramas, but when it comes to a church's loving welcome of committed gay couples, that's where they draw the line," says the Rev. Robert Chase, director of the UCC's communication ministry.

CBS and NBC's refusal to air the ad "recalls the censorship of the 1950s and 1960s, when television station WLBT in Jackson, Miss., refused to show people of color on TV," says Ron Buford, coordinator for the UCC identity campaign. Buford, who is African American, says, "In the 1960s, the issue was the mixing of the races. Today, the issue appears to be sexual orientation. In both cases, it's about exclusion."

In 1959, the Rev. Everett C. Parker organized UCC members to monitor the racist practices of WLBT. Like many southern television stations at the time, WLBT had imposed a news blackout on the growing civil rights movement, pulling the plug on then-attorney Thurgood Marshall. The Rev. Martin Luther King Jr. implored the UCC to get involved in the media civil rights issues. Parker, founding director of the UCC's Office of Communication, Inc., organized churches and won in federal court a ruling that the airwaves are public, not private property. That decision ultimately led to an increase in the number of persons of color in television studios and newsrooms. The suit clearly established that television and radio stations, as keepers of the public airwaves, must broadcast in the public interest.

"The consolidation of TV network ownership into the hands of a few executives today puts freedom of speech and freedom of religious expression in jeopardy," says former FCC Commissioner Gloria Tristani, currently managing director of the UCC's Office of Communication, Inc. "By refusing to air the UCC's paid commercial, CBS and NBC are stifling religious expression. They are denying the communities they serve a suitable access to differing ideas and expressions."

Adds Andrew Schwartzman, president and CEO of the not-for-profit Media Access Project in Washington, D.C., "This is an abuse of the broadcasters' duty to inform their viewers on issues of importance to the community. After all, these stations don't mind carrying shocking, attention-getting programming, because they do that every night."

The Rev. J. Bennett Guess is editor of *United Church News*, the national newspaper of the United Church of Christ.

About This Book

About the Associated Church Press

The oldest religious press association in North America, the Associated Church Press (ACP), founded in 1916, is an international community of communication professionals brought together by faithfulness to their craft and by a common task of reflecting, describing, and supporting the life of faith and the Christian community.

Among our purposes are:

1. To provide mutual support and encouragement, fostered by personal and professional relationships;
2. To promote higher standards of communication through professional growth opportunities and recognition of excellence;
3. To join in interfaith and public discourse with those who seek to build a more just society for all God's people.

Nearly two hundred publications, websites, news services, and individuals are ACP members, representing a combined circulation of several million.

The ACP annual competition draws more than a thousand entries from member publications, news services, and websites. This book includes some of the winners of the 2004 competition.

Learn more about the ACP at:

www.theacp.org

About the Award-Winning Publications

In print for more than 150 years, the *Adventist Review* is the flagship journal of the Seventh-day Adventist Church. Founded by James and Ellen White in 1849, the magazine is the one of the oldest religious publications in North America. The *Review* is published weekly and has a paid circulation of nearly 30,000.
 Learn more about the *Adventist Review* at:
 www.adventistreview.org

First published in 1843, **The Alabama Baptist** is a weekly newspaper of the Alabama Baptist State Convention that is mailed into about 110,000 Baptist homes in Alabama, providing a readership of more than a quarter of a million people. The paper is also mailed to subscribers in forty-eight states and the District of Columbia as well as to forty-eight different countries around the world. Each week *The Alabama Baptist* attempts to help empower Baptists to live out their Christian discipleship in their personal lives, their professional lives, and their lives within the community of faith. The paper provides concise and balanced reporting of events from the world of religion. Practical helps for everyday problems are provided. Moral and ethical issues are examined from a biblical standpoint. Resources for Christian living are shared.
 Learn more about *The Alabama Baptist* at:
 www.thealabamabaptist.org

Alliance Life is the official magazine of The Christian and Missionary Alliance. In 1882 Dr. A. B. Simpson, founder of The Christian and Missionary Alliance, began the denomination's official magazine to inform people about worldwide evangelism efforts and motivate readers to become involved in completing the Great Commission.

About This Book 153

Today the print magazine — and now the online version — touches lives with the wonderful message of Jesus Christ and with exciting accounts of Alliance mission activities around the world.

Learn more about *Alliance Life* at:
www.alliancelife.org

First published as the *Dominion Churchman* in 1875, **Anglican Journal** is the national newspaper of the Anglican Church of Canada. It has an independent editorial policy and is published by the Anglican Journal Board of Directors. The *Anglican Journal* is published monthly (with the exception of July and August) and is mailed separately or with one of 24 diocesan or regional publications.

Learn more about the *Anglican Journal* at:
www.anglicanjournal.com

Published monthly by the Christian Reformed Church in North America, **The Banner** magazine shows how the Christian faith in its Reformed expression makes sense for today's world. We believe that Jesus Christ calls us all to gratefully follow him in every area of life. That gives our daily living eternal significance and purpose. Whether we're addressing subjects like parenting, movies, politics, church ministries, or the society we live in, *The Banner* explores all such issues from the perspective of the good news that in Christ God is reconciling the world to himself. All who believe in Jesus are empowered by God's Spirit to serve as ambassadors of that reconciliation.

Learn more about the *The Banner* at:
www.thebanner.org

Formed at the suggestion of state paper editors, and supported with Cooperative Program (*www.cooperativeprogram.org*) funds, **Baptist Press News** (BP) has been the daily national news service of Southern Baptists since 1946. BP circulates to 40 state Baptist newspapers with a combined readership of 1.16 million and has a central bureau

in Nashville, as well as four active bureaus in Richmond, Virginia, Atlanta, LifeWay Christian Resources, and Washington.
Learn more about Baptist Press News at:
www.bpnews.net

ChristianNetworks.org was started in 1999 by Gordon McClellan as an outgrowth of his doctoral thesis proposal. It was Gordon's conviction that proper use of the Internet for Christian ministry could allow for the reaching of a truly worldwide audience while operating at a much lower cost than traditional ministries. The savings could then be directed to support Christian mission work throughout the world. This original concept has grown and matured. Today, the ***Christian Networks Journal*** is sold in over 380 bookstores throughout the United States and Canada.
Learn more about *Christian Networks Journal* at:
www.cnj.org

A Common Place is the bimonthly magazine of the Mennonite Central Committee. It brings you inspiring stories and spectacular photography as it introduces you to people around the world and the challenges they face.
Learn more about *A Common Place* at:
www.mcc.org/acp/

The Covenant Companion is the denominational magazine of the Evangelical Covenant Church. It seeks to inform, stimulate thought, and encourage dialogue on issues that impact the church and its members.
Learn more about *The Covenant Companion* at:
www.covchurch.org/communications/companion

The Cresset is a review of literature, the arts, and public affairs. It is published at Valparaiso University in Valparaiso, Indiana.
Learn more about *The Cresset* at:
www.valpo.edu/cresset

About This Book

DisciplesWorld is a journal of news, opinion, and mission for the Christian Church (Disciples of Christ). The name is drawn from that body of people — the Disciples of Christ — for and by whom it is published. The journal is an avenue for the expression of a wide variety of opinions, whether or not those opinions reflect some establishment or preferred viewpoint. It is the people's journal, written and read by laity and clergy alike and featuring articles on a wide spectrum of topics, along with Bible lessons, columns, media reviews, meditations, poetry, and short fiction. DisciplesWorld Inc. is a recognized organization of the Christian Church (Disciples of Christ), and reports to the denomination's General Assembly. But the magazine maintains organizational and editorial freedom in a journalistic tradition that has shaped Disciples' theology, character, and identity from the church's very beginnings.

Learn more about *DisciplesWorld* at:
www.disciplesworld.com

Episcopal Life is the national monthly newspaper of the U.S. Episcopal Church. Its mission is to inform, inspire, and involve the people of God by: reporting accurately and fairly events and issues in the Episcopal Church and the Anglican Communion, welcoming a healthy exchange of ideas and opinions among its readers, and nurturing the ministry to which all Episcopalians are called through baptism. Current circulation is 250,000.

Learn more about *Episcopal Life* at:
www.episcopal-life.org

Episcopal News Service (ENS) is the official news service of the Episcopal Church USA. Episcopal News Service content may be reprinted without permission as long as credit is given to ENS.

Learn more about ENS at:
www.episcopalchurch.org/ens/

The Lutheran is the magazine of the Evangelical Lutheran Church in America. Our editorial offices are in Chicago, and our publishing offices are located at Augsburg Fortress Publishers in Minneapolis. The magazine is a four-color monthly whose job it is to bring news of the church — local, national, and international — to the ELCA member. We strive to explore our Christian faith on a personal, congregational, and worldwide basis through stories that educate, inspire, and nurture faith.

Learn more about *The Lutheran* at:
www.thelutheran.org

Lutheran Woman Today, the magazine of Women of the Evangelical Lutheran Church in America, offers an exciting mix of faith-in-life articles, theological reflections, devotions, and stories of comfort and challenge that lift up the mission of Women of the ELCA: to mobilize women to act boldly on their faith in Jesus Christ. Each of the 10 issues per year will illuminate the path you travel as a person of faith and connect you to women both far and near who share a commitment to making God known. *Lutheran Woman Today* is published in partnership with Augsburg Fortress Publishers, the publishing house of the Evangelical Lutheran Church in America. Learn more about *Lutheran Woman Today* at:
www.lutheranwomantoday.org

The Mennonite is a semimonthly magazine for members of the Mennonite Church USA, an Anabaptist historic peace church. The mission of *The Mennonite* is to help readers glorify God, grow in faith, and become agents of healing and hope in our world. Our issues carry articles, news of the church (both national and international), commentary, letters, columns, and editorials.

Learn more about *The Mennonite* at:
www.themennonite.org

About This Book

Mennonite Weekly Review (MWR) is an inter-Mennonite newspaper published weekly since 1923. It is owned by Mennonite Weekly Review Inc., a nonprofit corporation in Newton, Kansas. MWR reaches a readership crossing conference and regional boundaries, mostly in the United States. MWR is an independent journalistic ministry not sponsored or subsidized by any conference or agency. The newspaper's income is derived from advertising and subscriptions. MWR exists to foster communication and cooperation within the Mennonite family of faith, encouraging support for the work of the church, its structures, and institutions. It seeks to be a medium for the preservation and spread of Christian beliefs and ideals as interpreted in the Anabaptist/Mennonite tradition.

Learn more about MWR at:
www.mennoweekly.org

Messenger traces its beginnings to 1851, when Henry Kurtz published the first issue of *The Gospel Visitor*. The next 30 years saw 33 more periodicals begun. Numerous consolidations and name changes occurred in the years leading up to 1883, when the first issue of *The Gospel Messenger* was published. It was considered the official church paper, though it was not actually owned by the church until 1897, when the church assumed ownership of the Brethren Publishing House. In 1965 the paper became a biweekly magazine, took on a completely new look, and shortened its name — to simply *Messenger*. Becoming a monthly magazine in 1973, *Messenger* continues to be the official magazine of the Church of the Brethren and is published in Elgin, Illinois, by the Church of the Brethren General Board.

Learn more about *Messenger* at:
www.brethren.org/genbd/messenger/

The **Presbyterian News Service** (PNS) is the official news agency of the Presbyterian Church (U.S.A.). Its job is to gather news and information about the denomination and its work and disseminate it to church members, church officials, religious and secular media, and the public. PNS is a news agency, not a public relations or promotional entity. As such it has editorial freedom to report fully and fairly on all aspects of the church, both good and bad.

Learn more about PNS at:

www.pcusa.org/news/

Presbyterians Today is the award-winning general-interest magazine of the Presbyterian Church (U.S.A.). Published 10 times a year, it explores practical issues of faith and life, tells stories of Presbyterians who are living their faith, and covers a wide range of church news and activities. *Presbyterians Today* features easy-to-understand articles about what Presbyterians believe, Bible study and devotional helps, and provocative commentary on the church's role in society.

Learn more about *Presbyterians Today* at:

www.pcusa.org/today/

For nearly seventy years, **Religion News Service**™ (RNS) has been an authoritative source of news about religion, ethics, spirituality, and moral issues. Based in Washington, D.C., RNS has a network of correspondents around the world, providing news and information on all faiths and religious movements to the nation's leading newspapers, news magazines, broadcast organizations, and religious publications. RNS's first priority is to provide intelligent, objective coverage of all religions — Judaism, Christianity, Islam, Asian religions, and private spirituality. RNS also provides commentary from a diverse array of all points of the political and theological spectrum.

Learn more about RNS at:

www.religionnews.com

Sojourners is a Christian ministry whose mission is to proclaim and practice the biblical call to integrate spiritual renewal and social justice. In response to this call, we offer a vision for faith in public life by: publishing **Sojourners Magazine,** *SojoMail,* and other resources that

About This Book

address issues of faith, politics, and culture from a biblical perspective; preaching, teaching, organizing, and public witness; nurturing community by bringing together people from the various traditions and streams of the church; hosting an annual program of voluntary service for education, ministry, and discipleship. In our lives and in our work, we seek to be guided by the biblical principles of justice, mercy, and humility.

Learn more about Sojourners at:
www.sojo.net

United Church News is the independent-voiced national news service of the 1.3-million-member United Church of Christ. In addition to its online edition, United Church News publishes a distinctive print edition six times annually. United Church News seeks to provide fair and accurate coverage for and about the UCC, its members, pastors, congregations, and the general public.

Learn more about United Church News at:
news.ucc.org

The United Church Observer is one of the oldest and most respected church publications in Canada. An independent denominational magazine, *The United Church Observer* reports on issues affecting denominational and congregational life within the United Church of Canada, as well as covering a wide range of general-interest issues of concern to people of faith today.

Learn more about *The United Church Observer* at:
www.ucobserver.org

***The United Methodist Reporter*,** founded in 1847 by a Methodist pastor in Brenham, Texas, serves the 10.3 million members of the global United Methodist Church. The weekly is the fifth-oldest continuously published newspaper in America. The *Reporter* covers news of interest to both clergy and lay United Methodists, maintains an open forum for dialogue reflecting the diversity of Christian viewpoints, and upholds a time-honored Wesleyan tradition: "We look upon the whole world as our parish."

Learn more about *The United Methodist Reporter* at:
www.umr.org

U.S. Catholic is a monthly forum for lay Catholics, covering issues of concern to Catholics in their everyday lives. *U.S. Catholic* is not afraid to tackle the controversial topics of our times. Recent issues have included reports and reader surveys on the death penalty, welfare reform, and America's culture of violence. *U.S. Catholic* celebrates Catholic tradition, yet embraces the spirit of Vatican II reform and rejuvenation. *U.S. Catholic* is published by the Claretian Missionaries.

Learn more about *U.S. Catholic* at:
www.uscatholic.org

Vital Theology is an independent ecumenical publication. We are not constrained by any institutional, denominational, or corporate influence. *Vital Theology* does not focus on news of the church. We are much more likely to provide theological views on the latest scandal in the mutual fund industry than to report on disputes within a particular denomination. *Vital Theology* provides: timely and concise theological interpretation of the news that makes headlines in the U.S. and around the world; theological "reads" on stories that are under-reported in the U.S. but which have a startling impact on people elsewhere; special reports that highlight the most interesting and useful information from major theological conferences; and book recommendations made by respected theologians from all parts of the theological spectrum.

Learn more about *Vital Theology* at:
www.vitaltheology.com

About This Book

Zion's Herald is an independent religious journal of opinion, news, and reflection. It is published bi-monthly by the Boston Wesleyan Association. The BWA is an autonomous organization of 20 lay people chartered by the Commonwealth of Massachusetts as a not-for-profit publisher of religious materials. In addition to publishing *Zion's Herald*, which it has done since acquiring publication rights in 1833, the Boston Wesleyan Association publishes books under the imprint of the BW Press. Although its heritage is rooted in the tradition of American Methodism, *Zion's Herald* is not related to any official body of the church. The BWA extends complete editorial freedom to its editors, guaranteeing an independent voice in the world of mainstream religious journalism. Zion's Herald has recently changed its name to *The Progressive Christian.*

Learn more about *Zion's Herald* at:

www.zionsherald.org